Designer        Chris Harrison
Art Director    Charles Matheson
Series Editor   James McCarter
Editor          Gregor Ferguson
Consultant      Charles Messenger
Researcher      John MacClancy

Illustrators    Peter Sarsens
                Rob Shone
                Andy Farmer

© Aladdin Books Ltd

Designed and produced by
Aladdin Books Ltd
70 Old Compton Street
London W1

Printed in Belgium

First published in the
United States in 1985 by
Franklin Watts
387 Park Avenue South
New York NY 10016

ISBN 531 04934 5

Library of Congress
Catalog Card No. 84-51810

The publishers would like to thank the following organizations and individuals for their help in the preparation of this book: Boeing Military Airplane Corporation; Bofors Ordnance; British Aerospace Company; British Ministry of Defence; DAVA; Ford Aerospace and Communications Corporation; General Dynamics Corporation; Hughes Aircraft Corporation; Jane's Publishing Company; Lockheed International; Martin Marietta; McDonnell Douglas Corporation; NASA; Royal Navy Public Relations Office; SNIAS; TASS; US Marine Reserve Public Relations Office; US Navy Public Relations Office; West German Department of Defence.

Photographic Credits:
4/5 Bofors; 8/9 Martin Marietta, Hughes; 10/11 Bofors, McDonnell Douglas; 12/13 USMR, US Navy, Lockheed; 14/15 DAVA, General Dynamics, Jane's, Ian V Hogg; 16/17 British Aerospace, TASS, SNIAS; 20/21 West German Department of Defence, Safrigal, Bofors, US Collection; 22/23 DAVA, F. Spooner; 24/25 British Ministry of Defence, Ian V Hogg; 26/27 Ian V Hogg; 28/29 Ian V Hogg, Ford Aerospace, TASS; 30/31 Ian V Hogg, Martin Marietta; 34 to 44 Ian V Hogg, The MacClancy Collection.

# 20th CENTURY WEAPONS

# MISSILES AND ARTILLERY

## IAN HOGG

## FRANKLIN WATTS

New York · London · Toronto · Sydney

# Introduction

The first recorded use of artillery was in AD 1326, when brass cannon and iron balls were manufactured for the defense of Florence, Italy. From then onward, artillery gradually became the principal military weapon, until by the Second World War some armies had more gunners than infantry soldiers.

But improvements in military aircraft and the arrival of the nuclear weapon and the guided missile all combined to reduce the importance of artillery during the next twenty years, bringing doubts whether artillery would survive at all. Then, the awareness of the full terror of unrestricted nuclear warfare made soldiers realize that there was still a need for weapons which could be employed in situations where nuclear weapons were too powerful, and in conditions where missiles could not operate. This has led to a growing concern with improved artillery weapons which can be fitted to specific types of warfare.

At the same time the guided missile has changed from being simply a long-range bombardment weapon into a system of weapons which can be designed to suit particular tasks: the missile which is designed for air defense is useless for land bombardment. Neither type would be much use for attacking armored vehicles. So subdivisions of missiles have made their appearance.

The result is that now missiles and artillery work together rather than in opposition. For some tasks the missile is ideal, for others artillery is best suited. Modern armies must therefore have a selection of both types of weapons.

## Mobility

The other great change in warfare over the past fifty years has been in mobility, the speed of the various parts of the army in moving and in carrying out their assigned roles. The self-propelled gun, in which the gun is carried on a tank or some other armored vehicle so as to be able to move as quickly across country as possible, forms a major part of most armies. Missiles are also provided with wheeled or tracked mountings so that they can keep up with the fast-moving thrust elements of the attack.

This book sets out not only to describe the various types of artillery and missile, but also to explain how the weapon is directed at its target, how it is operated, and how the various types of gun, howitzer and missile are fitted into the organizational framework of the army.

# Contents

| | |
|---|---|
| Missiles and Guns | 6 |
| Launch and Control Systems | 8 |
| Guidance Systems | 10 |
| Strategic Missiles | 12 |
| Short Range Missiles | 14 |
| Missiles versus Artillery | 16 |
| The Battlefield | 18 |

| | |
|---|---|
| Self - Propelled Guns | 20 |
| Artillery in Action | 22 |
| Ammunition | 24 |
| Light Artillery | 26 |
| Air Defense | 28 |
| Remotely Delivered Munitions | 30 |
| The Future | 32 |
| Missiles and Artillery: History and Development | 33 |
| Missiles and Artillery in Service Today | 45 |
| Glossary | 46 |
| Index | 47 |

**Above:** Swedish-made Bofors gun

# Missiles and Guns

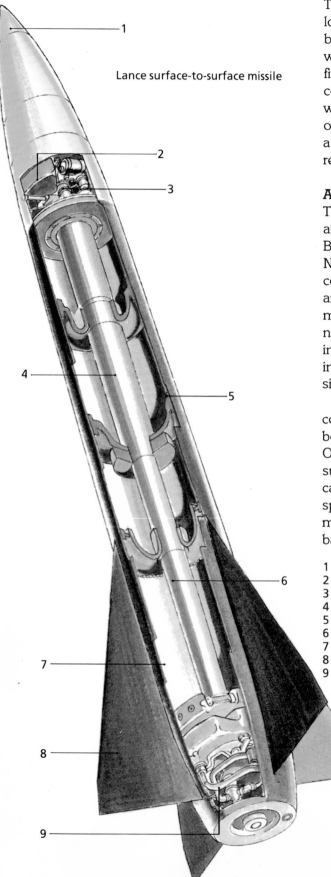

Lance surface-to-surface missile

1
2
3
4
5
6
7
8
9
13
14
10

The tactical guided missile is the field commander's long range weapon; the commander who wishes to bombard the enemy's cities has the ballistic missile, which can fly between continents. The army in the field merely needs something to hit the enemy command headquarters or supply dumps. These will be located well behind the front line so as to be out of range of artillery, but the tactical missile, with a range of perhaps 150km (98 miles) will be able to reach them quite easily.

## A tactical missile

The missile shown here, as an example, is Lance, an American design which is used by the USA, Britain, West Germany, Italy, Belgium, the Netherlands and Israel. Just over 6m (19 ft) long, it contains a warhead, a guidance package, fuel tanks and an engine. Two fuels are used, and these, when mixed in the motor, ignite and burn to give the necessary thrust to the rocket. The fuels are forced into the engine by gas produced by a generator inside the missile. Guidance is performed by a simple inertial spin torque system.

During the first part of its flight, the missile is controlled by directions for elevation and compass bearing, which are chosen and set before firing. Once the missile is on course for the target, the supply of fuel is cut off at the exact moment calculated to allow it to reach the target with the speed it already possesses. From then on the missile is no longer guided, and is said to be on a ballistic trajectory.

1 Warhead
2 Guidance system
3 Spin torque system
4 Solid propellant gas generator
5 Liquid fuel container
6 Liquid fuel transfer tube
7 Liquid oxidizer
8 Fin
9 Motors

## General support artillery

General support artillery is the term used to describe the guns and howitzers which provide the gunfire support for most military operations. The most commonly used type among western nations is the 155mm (6 in) howitzer. The one shown here is the FH-70, designed jointly by Britain, West Germany and Italy. It fires a shell weighing 43.5kg (96 lbs) to a maximum range of 24km (15 miles).

The weapon consists of a carriage, a recoil system and the ordnance or howitzer barrel. The carriage is a split trail: two legs which are spread so as to make a firm support together with the wheels. The recoil system contains oil-filled cylinders which allow the barrel to slide back under the force of firing, and compressed air cylinders which then push it back into the firing position. The barrel has a breech block, which is opened to allow the shell and cartridge to be loaded, and a muzzle brake which reduces the force of recoil. The carriage also has a small gasoline engine which provides power to the main wheels, and allows the gun to be driven short distances. Small "trail wheels" support the trail. The self-digging spades and soleplate give stability when the gun is fired.

## Maneuverability

The motor also provides power to elevate and swing the barrel and to load the shell. When traveling longer distances, the weapon is towed by a heavy truck which carries ammunition and the gun crew. The FH-70 can be unhooked and can start firing in less than two minutes.

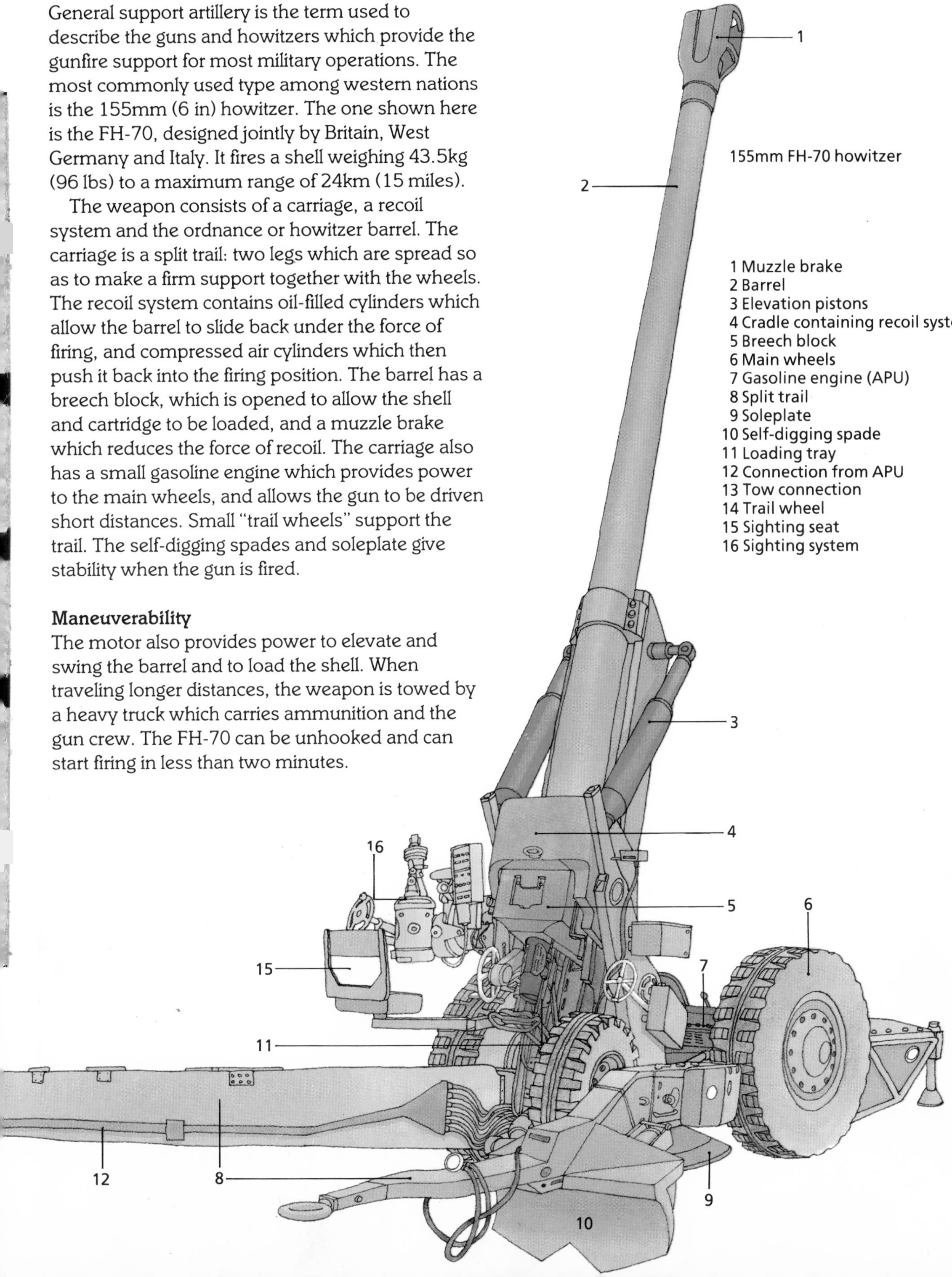

155mm FH-70 howitzer

1 Muzzle brake
2 Barrel
3 Elevation pistons
4 Cradle containing recoil system
5 Breech block
6 Main wheels
7 Gasoline engine (APU)
8 Split trail
9 Soleplate
10 Self-digging spade
11 Loading tray
12 Connection from APU
13 Tow connection
14 Trail wheel
15 Sighting seat
16 Sighting system

# Launch and Control Systems

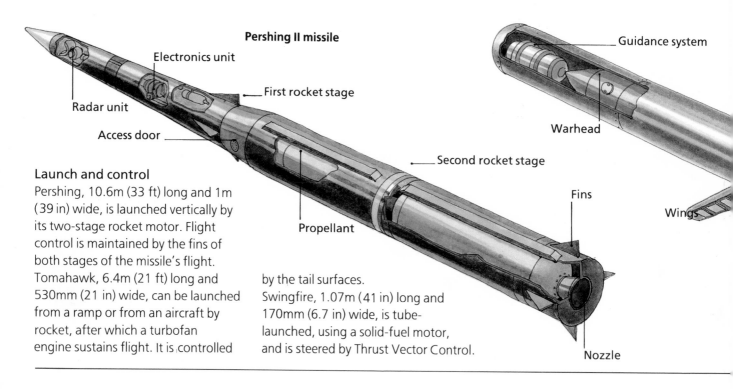

**Pershing II missile**

Electronics unit

Radar unit

Access door

First rocket stage

Guidance system

Warhead

Second rocket stage

Propellant

Fins

Wings

Nozzle

## Launch and control

Pershing, 10.6m (33 ft) long and 1m (39 in) wide, is launched vertically by its two-stage rocket motor. Flight control is maintained by the fins of both stages of the missile's flight. Tomahawk, 6.4m (21 ft) long and 530mm (21 in) wide, can be launched from a ramp or from an aircraft by rocket, after which a turbofan engine sustains flight. It is controlled by the tail surfaces.

Swingfire, 1.07m (41 in) long and 170mm (6.7 in) wide, is tube-launched, using a solid-fuel motor, and is steered by Thrust Vector Control.

Since the flight of the missile is guided, it is only necessary to support it during the launch and point it approximately in the right direction, as the guidance system within the missile itself will take care of the precise aiming.

Larger missiles are usually launched from a rail, with enough length to allow them to get up to flight speed before they leave its support. Very large missiles can be stood upright on their tails and allowed to take off under rocket power, straight up into the air. The guidance system then takes over when the missiles have gained sufficient speed.

## Doubling up

Smaller missiles, such as the majority of anti-tank and air defense weapons, are sealed into storage tubes in the factory. These tubes are also used as launch tubes, so that the missile is never exposed to damp air or damage during its life and never leaves its storage tube until it is fired. It is normal to use an extremely powerful boost motor rocket to get the missile into the air, after which a "sustainer" rocket or some other form of power (eg. a turbofan engine in the Tomahawk cruise missile) keeps up the flight speed.

Titan II ICBM, ground launched

TOW missile, mobile launched

Launch from underground silo

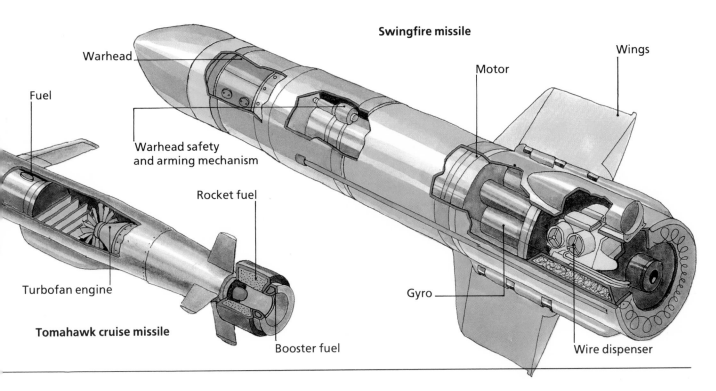

**Swingfire missile**

Warhead

Fuel

Warhead safety
and arming mechanism

Rocket fuel

Turbofan engine

Gyro

**Tomahawk cruise missile**

Booster fuel

Motor

Wings

Wire dispenser

### Steering in flight

Once in flight it is necessary to control the missile to steer it to the target. The electronic guidance system operates electrical or hydraulic devices which move the control systems. A missile with wings can be steered like an airplane, and can have moving surfaces on its wings to make it go up or down and a rudder to turn it to left or right. Alternatively, the wings can merely give lift and four tail surfaces can be used to steer and change its height. Missiles without wings, which move at high speed, use small fins to control their direction.

### Thrust Vector Control

Altering the direction of the rocket thrust is called Thrust Vector Control. This can be done by swiveling the motor. On smaller missiles such as Swingfire, the thrust can be deflected by sliding plates across the jet pipe.

The direction of the rocket thrust can also be changed by placing flaps in the rocket engine. As the flaps are moved, the direction is altered. Another method is to fit the missile with several small rocket jets which point outward around its body and fire these to swerve the missile.

### Thrust Vector Control

This method of steering the missile is by altering the direction thrust of the engine to one side or another. There are three modifications. The first is to use a jetevator. Here, there are two jets, operated by hydraulics, which can swing the thrust nozzle within the mounting. Secondly, moving flaps on either side of the thrust nozzle can alter the direction of the actual thrust. A third modification is by moving the entire thrust nozzle from one side to another by electronics.

Jetevator

Flaps

Electronics

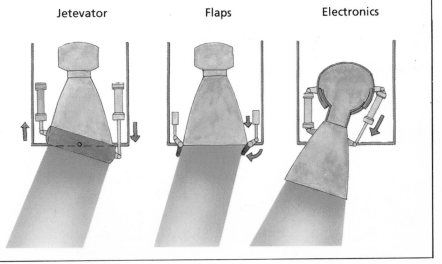

# Guidance Systems

There are two basic types of guidance: guidance to a remote location, used in ground-to-ground missiles, and homing onto a moving target, used by air defense missiles. The anti-tank missile is at present a cross-breed, using guidance to hit a moving target, but the next generation of anti-tank missiles will be similar to air defense missiles.

Guiding a missile to a specific location means knowing where the target is and where the missile is. These two must be expressed in the same terms; it is no use giving the map reference of the missile launcher according to your map, and the

Launching a light defense missile

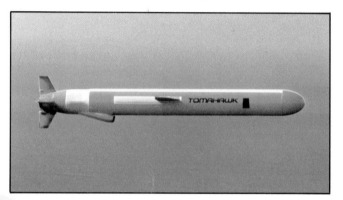

ALCM Tomahawk cruise missile in flight

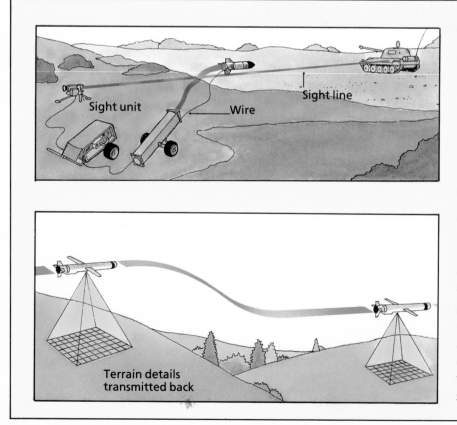

Sight line

Sight unit

Wire

Terrain details transmitted back

## Guidance by wire

The missile controller aims the sight at the tank and follows its course. The operater fires the missile, and this is programmed to fly into the sight line. The sight unit then measures the displacement and gives correcting commands by signals sent down the trailing wire.

## Terrain comparison

Inertial guidance can be backed up by terrain comparison (tercom). This is where the geographical features of the ground beneath the flight path are stored in the guidance computer's memory. Altimeters and TV cameras, also in the missile, keep a constant check on mountains, rivers and towns, comparing them with the stored information.

map reference of the target according to the enemy's map referencing system. For this reason, geographical coordinates (latitude and longitude) are usually preferred. Once these are known, it is possible simply to launch the missile, track it by radar, and steer it by radio commands, much as a model airplane is steered. But this system makes it very easy for the enemy to jam the controlling radio and take over control of the missile, perhaps steering it back to its launcher or to some harmless area. Even sending the orders in code is no defense, since modern computers can soon unravel any code.

The most effective method is "inertial guidance," in which the trajectory, or flight path, to the target is worked out by computer and fed into a memory in the missile itself. Gyroscopes then sense every movement of the missile as it flies, and constantly compare the trajectory being flown with the preset plan. Any deviation is immediately corrected, so that the missile follows the planned path.

## Homing systems

Homing against a moving target is done by using radar, an infrared detector or a TV camera in the missile. A radar homer sends out a radar signal, picks up the reflection from the target and steers the missile toward it. Infrared homers detect the heat given off by the target – a tank or aircraft engine – and, again, steer the missile to the strongest heat

Missile strike

source. TV cameras can be programmed with a picture of the target, then scan the area until they find a similar picture and, keeping this in the center of the picture, steer the missile toward it. Laser beams can also be used for homing.

## Wire guidance

Anti-tank missiles are controlled by signals sent out along a thin wire which is unwound as the missile flies. The operator keeps sight of the tank, and an infrared detector in the sight sees a flare in the missile tail. Any gap between the position of this flare and the direction in which the sight is pointed, can be measured, and corrections automatically sent down the wire steer the missile into sight.

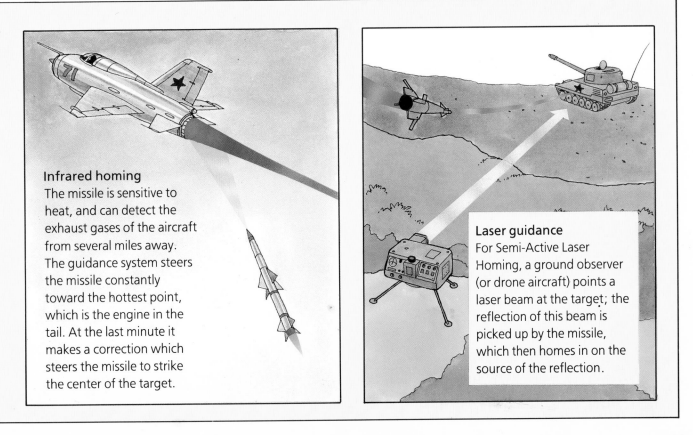

**Infrared homing**
The missile is sensitive to heat, and can detect the exhaust gases of the aircraft from several miles away. The guidance system steers the missile constantly toward the hottest point, which is the engine in the tail. At the last minute it makes a correction which steers the missile to strike the center of the target.

**Laser guidance**
For Semi-Active Laser Homing, a ground observer (or drone aircraft) points a laser beam at the target; the reflection of this beam is picked up by the missile, which then homes in on the source of the reflection.

# Strategic Missiles

Strategic missiles are those that are used by the highest commanders of the army, to bombard an enemy country at very long range; they are called strategic because their use affects the overall strategy of the war, whereas battlefield tactical missiles only affect the immediate outcome of a battle.

### Launch methods

Strategic missiles can be launched from land sites, ships, submarines or aircraft in flight. These options allow a commander to conceal missiles, mainly by having them on the move, so that their exact

Pershing missile being launched

position at any moment is not known to the enemy. But land-launched missiles are usually concealed in silos, deep pits which are camouflaged and scattered about the countryside. Sea-launched strategic missiles are usually carried in submarines; since these operate beneath the water it is difficult for an enemy to track them, and thus it would be possible to launch the missiles from under the water before the enemy was aware.

With land-sited missiles, the enemy may not know exactly where they are, but will have a rough idea and can keep a radar watch on the area. Therefore the enemy will know as soon as the missiles are launched, and take defensive measures. Air-launched missiles are carried by large aircraft, and can be launched from anywhere, but, again, these aircraft can be tracked by radar and the launch of the missile can be detected.

Depending upon the type, strategic missiles can have ranges of up to several thousand miles. In order to reach these distances, the rocket motor may be in a number of stages which ignite in succession to give additional boost, as the previous engine runs out of fuel and another takes over.

### A two-stage rocket

To reach its maximum range a Pershing II missile, for example, is launched using a boost motor. When this has burned out it falls away. A second motor, the sustainer, is then ignited, giving the missile thrust to the highest point of its flight. This then also falls away, leaving only the warhead, guidance and control systems in the rocket. As it nears the target, its terrain scanning radar checks the area against information in its own computer, before striking the target.

**Flight stages**

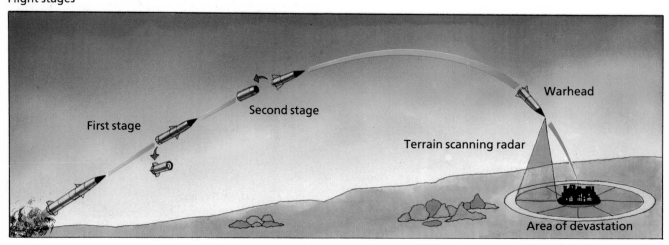

First stage

Second stage

Warhead

Terrain scanning radar

Area of devastation

MIRV

Trident I underwater missile launch

Nuclear warhead exploding

### Multiple re-entry warheads

In order to do the greatest damage with the least number of missiles, the multiple re-entry warhead splits up as it enters the atmosphere. The warhead then releases a number of smaller, independently programmed units. These have their own inertial guidance system and have been preset to fly to their own specific targets. These targets can be 160km (100 miles) or more apart.

### Warheads

Strategic missiles usually have nuclear warheads in order to obtain the greatest strategic effect from their use. However, if missiles with single warheads aimed at specific targets are used, a very large number of missiles would be needed to threaten a large country with many suitable targets. To provide as great a coverage as possible from the minimum number of missiles, the multiple re-entry warhead, or "Maneuverable Independently Targeted Re-Entry Vehicle" (MIRV) has been developed. Here the warhead contains a number of smaller warhead units, each of which has an independent guidance and control system.

### Travels through space

The name "Re-Entry Vehicle" comes from the fact that this type of missile leaves the Earth's atmosphere and "re-enters" as it approaches the target. As it does so, the main warhead opens and releases the multiple warheads, each of which is programmed to fly off on a separate course to its own pre-selected target.

In addition to causing the maximum of damage, this system also means that defense against the weapon is difficult, since a defense system will have to deal, not with a single missile, but with all the independent warheads. Moreover, some of these warheads can be dummies or decoys, to draw the defenses away from the real warheads or from another following missile.

# Short Range Missiles

Missiles used against tanks and low-flying aircraft have the advantage that their operators are often able to see their targets. They also have very specific targets, so that the warheads can be designed precisely for the task to be done. They need only be small, and therefore many of them can be hand-carried and even fired from the shoulder. The problem lies in guiding them.

## Short range guidance

A missile fired at one particular tank among several on the battlefield must be guided by its controller, since any current form of homing device might well home in on the wrong target. All ground based anti-tank missiles in current use are wire-guided, trailing a thin wire behind them which is connected to the sighting and control unit. Two types of control are used, Manual Command and Semi-automatic Command.

Manual Command means that the missile operator sights on the target and fires the missile; it is programmed to fly into the line of sight so that it is seen as it approaches the tank, and then the operator can actually steer it until it hits.

Semi-automatic Command means that the controller sights on the tank as before and fires the missile. But this time the sight is just moved to keep the tank on the cross-wires in the center. The missile has a flare in the tail and this flare is seen by an infrared detector in the sight. This measures the distance between the center of the sight and the missile, and then a computer works out the correction needed to steer the missile into the center of the sight and thus, directly toward the tank. The commands are sent down the wire automatically and the missile corrects itself. This continues until the missile strikes the target. An example of this is the TOW missile. TOW stands for Tube launched, Optically tracked, Wire guided, in other words a semi-automatic command, similar to the M-47 Dragon. Both TOW and Dragon can be mounted on the ground, vehicles or on helicopters.

## Homing systems

Command guidance has also been used for air defense missiles, with some success, but most of this type use infrared homing systems, such as the American Redeye. The missile is carried in a launch tube, on the operator's shoulder, and the sight unit contains a cooling system. When a target is seen, the operator aims the weapon and presses a switch. This starts the cooling system which cools down the infrared detector in the missile to −200°C, making it extremely sensitive to heat.

Within two or three seconds the detector will pick up the heat emitted by the target aircraft's engine, even at ranges as great as 5km (3 miles). Once the detector has locked on to the target, a buzzer

Redeye air defense missile being fired

Preparing to fire M-47 Dragon anti-tank weapon

Tank target hit by missile

TOW 2 missile launcher

sounds, and the operator then fires the missile. A small charge throws the missile clear of the launch tube, after which the main rocket motor ignites and the rocket accelerates. The detector is still locked on to the target and it transmits steering commands, guiding the missile to impact. As the missile approaches, a small correction is made to its flight path. This is because the hottest part of the aircraft is the engine tail pipe, and hitting this would do little damage. So the correction swerves the missile away from the tail pipe to hit the aircraft in its center, where it is more vulnerable to damage. The Redeye, though, is an earlier model, without the correcting ability. Therefore, it is at its best once the attack has finished, and the aircraft is leaving.

## Warheads

Anti-tank warheads use shaped charges, since this is the only way a low-velocity weapon can pierce armor plate. The focusing effect of the shaped charge makes the explosive jet blow a hole through thicknesses of up to 1m (3.6 ft) of hard armor. The Milan anti-tank missile, which has a daylight range of 3km (1.5 miles), has a shaped charge that can penetrate up to 500mm (20 in) and wreck the interior of the tank. Air defense missiles are used simply to cause a violent blast in order to smash the aircraft, and, therefore, use a maximum amount of high explosive in a simple steel warhead. They may be fused to detonate on impact, or be fitted with a proximity fuse.

Tactical sighting Milan

# Missiles versus Artillery

British FH-70 155mm howitzer

### Separate roles

The above picture shows a British FH-70 155mm howitzer. The FH-70 can fire six 43kg (95lb) shells every minute to a range of 24km (15 miles), and is used for the more day-to-day task of rapidly shelling troop concentrations across the front line.

Scud weighs 6.3 tonnes (6.2 tons) without its launch vehicle, has a range of about 250km (155 miles), and can fire once an hour. Each, obviously, has its own role to play. Scud can be used for seeking out and destroying something vitally important like an enemy communications headquarters or supply dump.

Missiles have to co-exist with artillery, because there are tasks for each which the other cannot perform. Missiles have the following advantages: they have a longer range; they can carry heavier warheads, and they can be controlled and guided throughout their flight.

Guns have other advantages: they can operate in any weather conditions, day or night; they are immune to any form of electronic countermeasure; they are much cheaper than a missile of comparable size, and they have a far higher rate of fire.

We can thus see, that if the problem is one of bombarding a city 3000km (1865 miles) away, the missile is the only possible solution, but if the target is only 25km (15 miles) away, then artillery can do the job more cheaply and, by firing several shots instead of one, can probably do the task more effectively than the missile.

An army commander in the field will therefore be provided with both missiles and artillery. The missiles will include the tactical battlefield bombardment missiles, the air defense and anti-tank missiles. The artillery weapons will include short-range close support light guns, possibly some anti-tank guns, air defense guns, medium-range general support howitzers, and perhaps some very long range guns, as well.

Soviet Scud missile carrier

### Guns and howitzers

The difference between a gun and a howitzer of the same caliber is, briefly, that a gun fires a shell on a fairly flat trajectory at high velocity, while a howitzer fires the shell on a high trajectory and at a low velocity so that it passes over intervening obstacles such as hills. The gun shell arrives from the front, and can be defended against; the howitzer shell drops steeply on to its target and it is very difficult to provide protection against.

### Coast defenses

Until the end of the Second World War, all countries with coastlines had large numbers of guns protecting their harbors and naval bases. When missiles came into use, most but not all of these coastal defense guns were dismantled, because it was reasoned that a jet or a missile could fly over them and wreck the protected area without being harmed. In recent years, however, it has been realized that there are other ways of damaging dockyards and that, for instance, ships at sea could lie some distance off and fire missiles at fairly short ranges. As a result, both guns for close artillery support and missiles are being used for coastal defense today.

The missile is preferred for this task because it can be made mobile. A coastal defense gun, once set down in position, can only defend the small area of its immediate vicinity. Defending a large area, therefore, demanded a large number of guns and a large number of crews to operate them. But a mobile coastal defense missile can be parked at some convenient central spot and moved at short notice, with only a small crew needed, to go to any required position.

6 inch caliber coastal defense gun

### Protecting the coast

Above is a 6 inch coast gun at Gibraltar, one of the few specimens of that type of weapon. Below, is the French Exocet missile launcher, carrying four missiles. This has a range of 70km (46.5 miles). It is guided in two phases: inertial and a radar homing system. The Exocet coastal defense system has been adopted by the armed forces of several countries.

French Exocet missiles

# The Battlefield

The diagram below shows, in representative form, how the various weapons are deployed on the battlefield and roughly where they are located in respect to the front line. For clarity, the front line is shown as the river which divides the scene. On the right is, an attacking force, and on the left the weapons of the defensive force.

A river is a natural obstacle, since it can be crossed only by using existing bridges or by bringing up specialized equipment such as mobile bridges, ferries, or amphibious tanks and vehicles. Therefore, it is a good place for a defensive force to make its stand, and here the forward elements are spread out along the river bank.

For immediate defense there are infantrymen with rifles and machine guns, and, scattered throughout their ranks, short-range anti-tank guided missiles (1) and anti-tank artillery (2). In order to keep a constant watch on the enemy's movements and report them back to the commanders, there are short-range radar sets (3) and forward observers for the artillery (4).

## High-tech vision

These observers will be provided with small computer terminals into which they can key information, which is then transmitted to a master computer which re-transmits the information to artillery batteries. The artillery observers will use optical instruments such as binoculars and night vision devices, and laser rangefinders to measure the location of targets.

Also close to the first line of the defenders, will be soldiers carrying short-range air defense missiles (5), such as Blowpipe or Stinger to protect the front line troops from air attack. Aircraft, which pass over these defenses with the intention of attacking targets further back, will meet the air defense missiles (6), such as Rapier, as well as light air defense guns (7), protecting the rear areas.

Behind the first line of defense, situated where it can see as much as possible, will be one or more long-range battlefield surveillance radar (8), looking deep into enemy territory and capable of detecting the movement of any type of vehicle or weapon.

Battlefield tactics

There will also be special radar to detect the flight of shells or mortar bombs, analyze the trajectory, and calculate the position of the gun or mortar which fired them; this location will then be fed into the computer system and sent to the artillery so that they can bombard these targets.

Further back – perhaps some 3km (1.8 miles) behind the front line – we find the close support artillery (9) concealed in the forward edge of a wood from which they can give covering fire to the front troops. These are usually 105mm (4 in) howitzers or guns and can be moved very quickly, to prevent their being detected or attacked.

Further back still – 5km (3 miles) or so – is the general support artillery (10), in this case a battery of self-propelled 155mm (6 in) howitzers, and the multiple launch rocket system (11), both of which can be employed on the instruction of the forward observers to bombard and break up enemy formations preparing to attack. The multiple launch rocket system can fire projectiles which dispense sub-munitions in an air-burst (12) above the target

area. These sub-munitions can be contact mines strewn in the path of advancing tanks. Right at the rear are the tactical missiles (13) which can be fired against specified targets deep behind enemy lines.

### Detecting the targets

Detecting these targets is, of course, the hardest part of the battle, since the enemy will go to great lengths to conceal their movements and assembly as long as possible in order to create surprise. One way to find targets is to employ a pilotless aircraft or drone (14) which, controlled by radio, can be flown over enemy territory. Fitted with a TV camera, it can observe the ground underneath and immediately signal back what it sees to monitor screens in the headquarters. The drone can also be fitted with infrared detectors or special line-scan radar equipment so that it can detect movement at night.

All these various elements are connected to each other by secure (from the enemy) radio and computer links. This means that all the information can be passed rapidly to everyone who needs it.

# Self-Propelled Guns

A self-propelled (SP) gun is a normal artillery piece but carried on a motorized mounting so that it can move quickly around the battlefield. It is usually mounted on a tank chassis, but some countries have wheeled SP guns such as the Swedish Bofors. But, although they are tracked and armored, they are not intended to drive into action with the tanks. Their role is the same as that of towed artillery, and their extra mobility is simply so that they can keep up with the movement of armored formations.

## Its own power

Carrying the gun on a motorized chassis means that power is available to swing the turret, elevate the gun and load the shells. Locating the gun inside the turret means that the crew is well protected against enemy gunfire. The gun carries a radio so that orders can be received directly, and modern guns carry computers which allow them to calculate their own firing data, making it possible for guns to operate individually, if required. Power assistance allows a high rate of fire to be achieved. Most SP guns can fire off a burst of six shots in less than one minute, after which they can start up and drive off immediately, causing any retaliatory fire to fall on empty ground.

Lack of space means that only a limited amount of ammunition can be carried – usually 40 rounds – and it is necessary to provide an armored support vehicle to carry extra ammunition.

155mm SP howitzer of the West German army

American M109AI SP gun

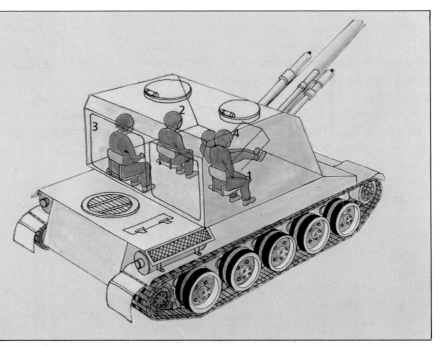

**The French GCT 155 howitzer**
This self-propelled weapon is fully automated and needs only a crew of four to operate it. The gunlayer (1) aims the weapon by electric power. The gunner (2) loads and fires. This is done by controlling a mechanical feed system which takes ammunition from racks, in the rear of the turret, and loads the shells, untouched by hand. The commander (3) controls the activity, and can relieve the other two for periodic rests. The driver (4) can also take over the duties of either crew when not required to drive.

Swedish FH-77 155mm howitzer

## Heavy towed artillery

The modern heavy towed gun is an extremely complicated piece of equipment, since it is expected to perform as well as a self-propelled gun, but without the compact turret, and without power from the vehicle engine. The models shown here are the Swedish FH-77 155mm howitzer and the South African G5 155mm.

The carriage is of the split trail type, with two main gun wheels and two smaller trail wheels on the trail legs. In front of the gun wheels is an auxiliary power unit (APU) with a Volvo gasoline engine driving hydraulic pumps. These hydraulic pumps drive motors in the main wheels, allowing the gun to drive under its own power at 8km/h (5 miles/h).

The gun can be steered by varying the speed of the main wheels, slowing down one and speeding up the other. For long distances, the gun is towed by a heavy truck, and the truck driver can, from the cab, switch on the gun's APU to provide additional power by driving the gun wheels when crossing difficult terrain, such as deep mud or snow.

## Preparing the gun

To put the gun into action, it is first uncoupled from the tractor by lowering the trail wheels, and then using hydraulic power to lift the trail. The right gunwheel is raised, tipping the gun and allowing the right trail leg to swing out. Then the right wheel is lowered and the left raised to swing the left leg out. The gun is reversed so that spades on the trail legs dig into the ground. The barrel is elevated and moved from left to right by hydraulic power.

Ammunition is hoisted by a hydraulic crane to the loading table behind the breech; three shells and cartridges are placed on the table and the loader operates an automatic rammer to load one cartridge and shell in one movement. The gunlayer fires the gun, the empty cartridge case is ejected as the gun recoils and the loader loads another round. All three rounds can be fired in eight seconds.

## The operators

There is a crew of six in the detachment. The gun commander, the gunlayer, who also drives the gun when using the auxiliary power unit, and the loader who operates the rammer. The ammunition handler places the cartridges on the loading table, while the crane operator places the shells. Another ammunition handler unboxes and prepares the ammunition for loading. The gunlayer and the loader are seated on the left and right sides of the gun, the remaining crew stand.

South African 155mm G5 howitzer

# Artillery in Action

An artillery battery rarely sees the target at which it is shooting; the guns are usually set well back from the front line and in concealed positions, so that their movements are hidden from the enemy. This, coupled with the long range at which shooting is conducted, makes direct vision impossible. It is therefore necessary to build an organization to ensure the guns are pointed in the right direction and that the accuracy of the fire can be confirmed.

When guns go into action they have a rough idea where their targets are likely to be, and they then pick a position accordingly. Once in the area, the first task is to calculate their location very exactly, to within 1m (3.6 ft), and establish where the compass point North lies. This is done by special survey troops who calculate the position from information already known about the locality, or they have electronic instruments which allow North to be determined.

The guns then select some prominent landmark and measure its angle from North. The gun sights are set at this angle and the guns moved until the sights point at the aiming point, which then means the gun barrels are pointing North.

### Finding the Target

Forward observers (1) radio back the target's position (2) relative to North, or key it in on a computer terminal (3). The gun is trained to this angle (shown blue) and elevated to the angle required to reach the target (shown red). Due to local conditions, such as wind (4) or temperature, the first shot misses (5). The observers report where this shot lands and corrections are made for a second shot (6). A final correction is needed before the true range is found (7).

Spotters in NATO exercise

### Finding the target

The forward observer, who is on the front line with the infantry and armor, and in the best place to see into enemy territory, now sees a target. With a laser rangefinder to measure its range, and a compass to determine its direction, the observer can work out the target's position from these figures on a map. This information is then radioed to the guns, or keyed into a computer terminal which passes it to the artillery.

At the gun position, another computer receives the target information. It already knows the gun's position, and by simple trigonometry can work out the direction, and range of the target, from the guns. The direction is given by setting the angle that the target makes from North on to the sight, then moving the gun barrel until the sight comes back on to the aiming point. The range is set by elevating the gun barrel, using a type of spirit level, to the angle which has been calculated to launch the shell so that it travels the right distance. This angle is found by extensive firing during trials.

### Adjustment for weather conditions

It is important to adjust the calculated range to allow for weather conditions. The computer's figures are calculated for a gun standing on level ground, firing at a standard temperature and barometric pressure and with no wind. If the temperature or pressure are different, and if there is a wind blowing, then the flight of the shell will be affected, and the computer must work out any difference and make the adjustments accordingly. A strong wind blowing straight toward the gun, for example, would mean that the gun must fire as if at a target which is further away.

### The final touches

Having fired the first round, the gunners wait for the forward observer to see where the shell landed. Since the observer's position may not know where the gun is, they can only say where the shell landed in relation to the target as they see it – for example, "200 meters too far, 150 meters to the left." The forward observer signals this back and the computer, which knows where the position is, in relation to both the gun and the target, can work out what correction is necessary to aim the shell on to the target. This is passed to the gun which fires its second shot. This should be close enough to the target for one final correction, and the observer orders "Fire for Effect." After this, all guns open fire, using the figures worked out by the ranging gun and the computer. The number of rounds they fire will have been ordered by the forward observer, and depends on the target's size and importance.

Checking the elevation

SP battery in action, Syria

# Ammunition

The artillery's weapon is the shell; the gun is simply a method of getting it to its target. The standard shell for all guns and howitzers is the high explosive shell; this is made of steel and filled with TNT or RDX explosive. Fitted with a fuse to detonate the explosive at the proper moment, it shatters the steel casing, creating large fragments and allows the blast and fragments to escape to damage the target. The shell is shaped to pass through the air smoothly. It has a driving band which grips the rifling of the gun and spins the shell so that it stays point-foremost as it flies through the air.

### Carrier shells

These are shells which contain various substances which have special effects at the target. The most common type is the smoke shell. This usually contains a filling of phosphorus which, when the shell breaks open gives off smoke. Alternatively it can have several canisters filled with chemicals which are thrown out over the target, fall to the ground and there give off smoke clouds. The object is to make a screen so that the enemy cannot see what is going on. Other carrier shells can have incendiary composition (for setting fire to the target) or a brilliant flare suspended on a parachute so as to illuminate the battlefield at night.

A modern type of shell is the sub-munition shell which is hollow and loaded with a number of small bombs. These are released over the target and fall in a scattered pattern. They are specially designed to attack tanks by piercing the thinner armor on top surfaces, and they also produce fragments and blast to injure any infantry in the locality. Another

Loading a 175mm SP gun

type of filling consists of anti-tank or anti-personnel mines, which can be scattered in front of an advancing enemy force.

For shooting at tanks, a special shell is used. This is the HEAT (High Explosive, Anti-Tank) shell. In its nose is a cone of copper, behind which the explosive is packed. When the shell strikes the tank the explosive inside detonates. The shaping of the copper cone focuses the blast of the explosive, rather like a lens focuses light into a beam. The blast forms a thin jet of explosive gas and molten copper which forces a small hole through the thickest armor.

### Cartridges and fuses

Cartridges are made of a special explosive which burns rapidly and generates a vast amount of gas to force the shell out of the gun. This explosive may be inside a brass case, or it may be in a cloth or plastic bag. The type of fuse in the shell is chosen according to its operation. It may burst the shell as it strikes the target, or have a short delay to allow the shell to go through a wall and burst inside, or it can be fitted with a timing device so that the shell bursts in the air over the target. The most effective fuse today is the proximity fuse, a tiny radar set which can detect the ground and automatically detonates the shell at the most effective height. This type of fuse is also used on some missiles to detect, for example, aircraft targets.

155mm shells in supply vehicle

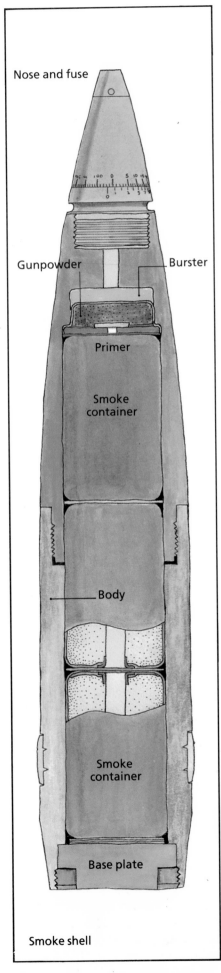

Nose and fuse

Gunpowder

Burster

Primer

Smoke container

Body

Smoke container

Base plate

Smoke shell

White phosphorus shell bursting in front of smoke screen

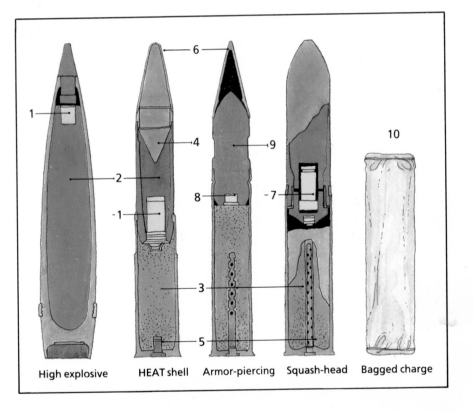

High explosive    HEAT shell    Armor-piercing    Squash-head    Bagged charge

## A smoke shell

The base ejection smoke shell has three loose canisters within its body that contain a smoke composition. The time fuse in the nose of the shell ignites a small gunpowder charge which activates the burster. The burster then flashes through the percussion primer in the central tube to light the canisters. The pressure of the explosion then blows the smoke canisters out of the shell.

## Ammunition types

(Left to right) High explosive shell; HEAT shell with cartridge; armor-piercing shot with cartridge; squash-head shell, and cartridge and a bagged propelling charge.
Shell details: 1 Fuse, 2 Bursting charge, 3 Propelling charge, 4 Copper cone, 5 Percussion primer, 6 Wind shield, 7 Base detonating fuse with tracer, 8 Tracer, 9 Solid steel shot, 10 Bag of propelling charge.

# Light Artillery

Light, or close support, artillery is used to accompany troops and provide immediate firepower to support their actions. It is light so that it can be transported into any position, by manpower if necessary, in order that the support the infantry needs is not denied to them.

## Mobility

In past years, it was customary to design small guns which could be dismantled rapidly and carried on the backs of mules, particularly in mountainous areas. Some countries, such as the forces in Afghanistan, still have mule-pack batteries. Most armies now rely upon modern helicopters to take artillery into inaccessible places and to move light guns about at high speed. With helicopters it is possible to move a six-gun artillery battery, its crew, ammunition and equipment, 10km (6.2 miles) and have it in ready to fight within half an hour. Because of its mobility, the British 105mm Light Gun was deployed in the Falklands War in 1982, where it proved very successful.

## Pack artillery

Pack guns are designed to be taken to pieces in two or three minutes, to be divided into loads which can be carried by one mule or two soldiers. They must be capable of being put together again in the same time. One of the most common pack weapons in use today is the Italian M56 105mm howitzer which dismantles into 11 loads, none weighing more than 120kg (250 lbs), in three minutes. It fires a 14kg (30 lbs) shell to a range of 10.5km (6.5 miles).

The pack gun was the obvious choice for airborne troops, since the individual components could be dropped by parachute and assembled quickly on the ground. As the technique of parachute-dropping was improved, it became possible to drop guns complete, and now pack weapons are in less use by airborne forces. They are still used by countries with mountainous areas which need to be protected or in which it may become necessary to operate; the Soviet army is currently using pack guns in Afghanistan.

## Airborne guns

Light artillery is chosen when very close support of infantry is needed. The American 105mm M102 howitzer (left) is seen in use by airborne troops, while the Italian 105mm M56 (below) is being fired at point-blank elevation against tank targets. Both weapons can be dropped by parachute, and the M56 can be dismantled into eleven loads for carriage by mules or for parachute drop from light aircraft.

American 105mm M102 howitzer

Italian 105mm M56

British 105mm pack howitzer

Puma helicopter lifting 105mm gun

## Light guns

The British Army used the Italian pack howitzer for several years after their 105mm became the NATO standard caliber for close support guns, and until it could develop a suitable gun of its own. Their principal objections were firstly that the pack howitzer was too fragile to withstand long distance towing behind a truck, and secondly that the ammunition (an American design) was no longer of the most modern type.

The 105mm Light Gun, developed in the 1970s, fires a new type of ammunition of much greater power and destructive effect to a range of 17km (10.5 miles). It has been designed to be as light, but as strong, as possible and uses special light alloys for much of the carriage. It weighs only 1858kg (4000 lbs) and can be carried into action slung beneath a Puma helicopter.

The 105mm Howitzer M102 is the American equivalent of the British Light Gun; it weighs even less – 1496kg (3300 lbs) – but still uses ammunition of pre-war design and can only achieve a range of 14.6km (9 miles), significantly less then the British gun. It can be carried under a Sikorsky Blackhawk helicopter. Both the M102 and the M56 fire the same ammunition and are widely used by the NATO forces.

Although Soviet policy has always stressed light weight in relation to performance, it is notable that the comparable Soviet gun, the 100mm BS-3, weights 3650kg (8000 lbs) but has the slightly longer range of 21km (13 miles).

## Moving guns

The helicopter has replaced the mule as the best method of moving artillery in difficult country. The British 105mm Light Gun (top) has a carriage of light alloy, it can be carried by the Puma and similar helicopters. The photograph (top right) shows a Puma lifting the 105mm gun during a NATO exercise.

## Mountain guns

Countries with mountains still have special light artillery for use in support of mountain troops. The Soviet 76mm M1927 (right) can be dismantled into pack loads. The trailer is only used when the gun is being towed on roads.

Soviet 76mm M1927 infantry gun

# Air Defense

German Twin 128mm gun

American Sergeant York

Air defense shooting is different to other types of artillery fire because the target is small, fast, and can appear from any direction, and at any altitude. As a result the guns must be fast-firing, very quick in moving to pick up a target, and must have very complicated sights to compensate for the movement of the target. The basic problem is that the shell takes some time to reach the target, by which time it has flown a considerable distance.

Air defense guns are usually of small caliber – up to about 40mm (1.6 in) – and can fire up to 250 shots per minute, so putting up a stream of shells to intercept the aircraft. Although the shells are small, the target is relatively fragile and one 40mm (1.6 in) shell is quite sufficient to do severe damage to a modern aircraft. The fuses must also be fitted with

some means of exploding the shell in the air should it miss the target, since it would be dangerous to allow the shell to fall back to the ground and explode.

Sighting systems for modern guns incorporate a computer. This measures the course and speed of the aircraft and calculates the amount of aim-off required; it then shifts the aiming mark in the sight and the gunner must then move the barrel until the aiming mark is back on the target. This throws off the barrel so that it is aimed ahead of the aircraft. Many guns also carry a radar set which scans the area and detects targets some distance away. This gives the gun crew warning and allows them to swing the gun in the right direction and be ready to pick up the target in the optical sight.

## Point defense

Point defense means defending a particularly important target such as a supply depot, refinery or ammunition factory. The defensive plan will cover every direction from which attack might come, and constant watch will be kept by radar sets (1). When these detect the approach of a target the missiles, such as Rapier (2) and guns (3) will be alerted. The missiles will first try to hit the attackers at long range, and the guns act as "back-stop" for targets which evade the missiles.

Soviet SA4 Ganef air defense missiles

American Chaparal mobile air defense missiles

### Air defense tanks

One of the principal enemies of the tank today is the missile-armed helicopter. Accordingly, certain armies are now adopting self-propelled air defense guns which can travel in company with tanks and protect them from air attack. The German and Dutch armies use Gepard, a German Leopard tank chassis with twin 35mm (1.4 in) guns and two radars, one for early warning and one for tracking the target and directing the guns while the US Army has adopted the Sergeant York, a tank chassis carrying a turret with two 40mm (1.6 in) automatic guns and radar. Like air defense missile systems they use radars, both to acquire the target and to pass directions to the missile, once launched, in order to hit it.

### Air defense missiles

Air defense missiles may be of two types: short range weapons fired from the shoulder, and intended to defend against low level attackers; and larger weapons fired from heavy launchers and capable of dealing with aircraft targets up to the highest altitudes. The Soviet SA-4 Gavel missile is launched and guided by radio command with a semi-active terminal homing phase for the final stage. The American Chaparal is an infrared homing missile; the operator launches the missile which then operates under its own internal power. The American Patriot and British Bloodhound II are examples of larger missiles fired from ground or self-propelled launchers and capable of dealing with targets over a wider area.

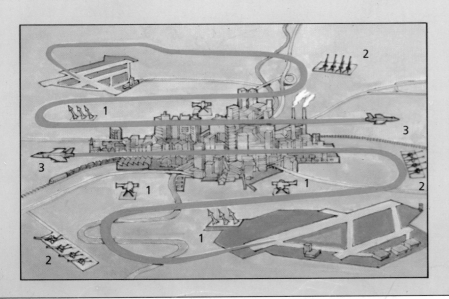

### Area defense

Area defense means spreading the defenses out in order to prevent attacks on a large area such as a major city. As with point defense, it means ringing the area with a mixture of missiles (1) and guns (2), the missiles for long range protection and the guns for dealing with whatever escapes the missiles. Interceptor and fighter aircraft (3) fly constant patrols across likely approach routes. This defense is against aircraft, but it is also possible to defend against incoming missiles.

# Remotely Delivered Munitions

## The Multiple-Launch Rocket System

The American Multiple-Launch Rocket System (MLRS) is carried on a tracked vehicle and consists of a launcher unit which is loaded with two sealed six-rocket pods. The entire operation of the system is computer-controlled. The location of the target is supplied by radio, and the computer calculates the firing data, basing it on its own position as given by special electronic equipment in the vehicle. The computer automatically raises and aims the rocket launcher and fires. The empty pods are then mechanically removed from the launcher and two fresh pods installed ready for the next engagement.

The rocket warhead is hollow and contains 644 dual-purpose bomblets packed in polystyrene foam. These bomblets weigh 0.23kg (0.5 lb) each and have both a shaped charge for penetrating armor and fragmentation casings for anti-personnel effect. Twelve rockets with these warheads can saturate an area of one sq km (0.4 sq mile) with 7728 bomblets. The chances of a tank escaping are very small.

An alternative warhead, under development in West Germany, carries 28 anti-tank mines; the rocket is fired so as to scatter these mines in the path of the tanks. This obstacle will cause the tanks to halt, while attempting to find a way through or around the mines, whereupon they become an excellent target for the bomblet warhead.

## Terminal guidance

When the tanks come within sight of forward observers or drone aircraft, it becomes possible to introduce a form of guidance. The Copperhead terminally guided artillery shell is fired from a 155mm (6 in) howitzer in the usual way and flies for most of its range as a normal shell. But, when it approaches the target area, it folds out a set of steerable fins and switches on a laser detector. Down on the ground, the observer has a laser projector which is directed at the target. Some of the laser energy is reflected and is picked up by the approaching shell. A microcomputer then steers the shell toward the source of the laser reflections, using the steerable fins, until the shell strikes the tank. The laser illumination can also be done by a remotely controlled drone aircraft.

Another method of terminal guidance is to build detectors into the bomblets. For this task a new type of radar, using a wavelength of only a few millimetres is being tried; this detects the tank

Missile launcher

because metal reflects the radar more strongly than the surrounding earth. The bomblets are carried in an artillery shell or a rocket, and ejected close to the target. They are suspended by parachutes and spin slowly as they descend, the radar seeking a target. Once it detects a target, it primes the warhead and fires it just as the spin brings it into line with the tank below. The explosion of the warhead fires a slug of steel downward and through the top surface armor of the tank.

Multiple Launch Rocket System MLRS 2

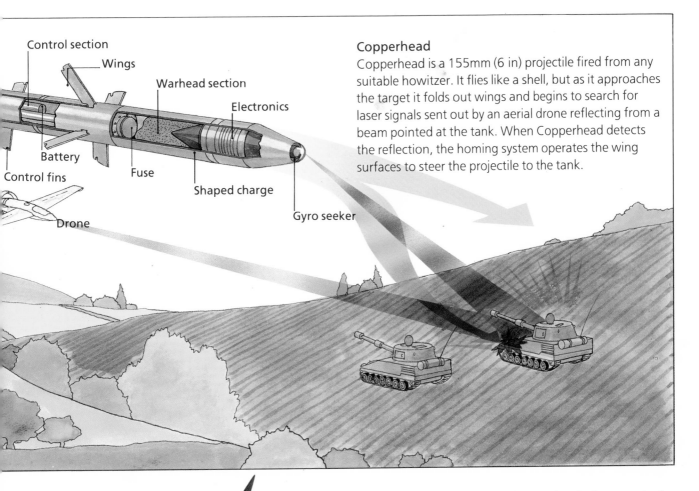

Control section
Wings
Warhead section
Electronics
Battery
Control fins
Fuse
Shaped charge
Gyro seeker
Drone

## Copperhead

Copperhead is a 155mm (6 in) projectile fired from any suitable howitzer. It flies like a shell, but as it approaches the target it folds out wings and begins to search for laser signals sent out by an aerial drone reflecting from a beam pointed at the tank. When Copperhead detects the reflection, the homing system operates the wing surfaces to steer the projectile to the tank.

Air Defense and Anti-Tank System   ADATS

The British Rapier is an example of a larger missile fired from ground or self-propelled launchers and capable of dealing with targets over a wider area. Modern tactics, particularly when confronted with a very strong attacking force of tanks, are aimed at engaging the enemy as deep within its own territory as possible. Artillery and missiles can be used at long range, but the effect of an individual shell or warhead against a mass of tanks several miles away is largely a matter of luck. As a result, methods of improving the chance of doing significant damage are now being adopted.

## ADATS

The Air Defense Anti-Tank System is a totally new hybrid that combines air defense and anti-tank technologies in a single battlefield weapon with a true dual capability. Each autonomous unit includes eight ready-to-fire, supersonic, self-contained missiles and an integral radar/electro-optical fire-control system. It can be mounted on a variety of ground vehicles. The photograph on the left shows the ADATS missile being fired.

# The Future

Prophecy is dangerous, but we can perhaps see what the future may bring by considering what is being developed today. The Warsaw Pact armies have four or five tanks to every one that NATO has, so one of the most important priorities is the development of an anti-tank missile which will find its own target and does not have to be wire-guided. The biggest problem is making sure the missile homes in on the target and does not home in on a tank which has already been knocked out.

### Air defense and artillery
Guns for short range air defense are making more progress than missiles at present. The short range missile is expensive, though because of the infra-red homing system, fire-and-forget is working well in this area. But modern guns can fire very rapidly, and with advanced computer technology their sights are extremely accurate. Gun ammunition is far cheaper than a missile, and with tiny proximity fuses even a shell which misses the target can still do damage if it passes close enough to operate the fuse.

Designs for new towed and self-propelled guns appear every year. There is an increasing tendency to develop the howitzer and turret as a separate assembly which can be fitted to the hull of any main battle tank in place of its normal turret. New designs of wheeled vehicles with improved cross-country performance are leading to their adoption as platforms for artillery, and a wheeled chassis is generally cheaper to build than a tracked one.

### Space Warfare
The most advanced field of missile technology promises to take the war out of the Earth's atmosphere and place it in space. It will soon be within our capabilities to put space stations, armed with weapons, into orbit so that they can, when required, destroy satellites and also deal with strategic missiles as they pass out of the Earth's atmosphere during their flight. The principal difficulty lies in the development of weapons, since ordinary artillery and rockets would be of little use in space. The favored weapon is the laser, using vast quantities of power which can destroy whatever the beam touches. Such weapons are not practical on Earth, since they would be so huge as to be immobile. But, weightless, in space, they could be built as large as necessary.

Space warfare for the future?

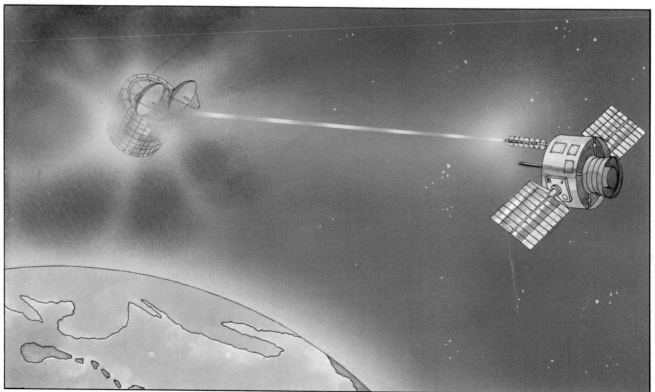

# Missiles and Artillery History and Development

Artillery began in the 14th century, with simple cast cannons firing stone balls and darts. Today, almost six hundred years later, we have weapons which, by means of computers, can actually aim and fire themselves.

Almost all the development of artillery has taken place in the past 150 years; until that time the cannon remained a smooth-bore muzzle loader firing a cannon-ball, although the manufacture and finish of the weapon had improved. But a gunner of the 14th century would have found nothing to baffle him in the artillery at Waterloo in 1815.

## Beginning of modern developments

The Crimean War (1854) led to great changes; infantry began to use rifles, with more range than the smooth-bore artillery, so rifled artillery had to be developed. Iron armor began to be used in forts and warships, so powerful guns were needed, and these became so long that breech-loading had to be adopted in about 1880. To make the guns less ponderous, they were made from a number of steel tubes, one upon another in layers to give the desired strength, instead of a bored-out lump of cast iron. But as guns became more powerful, so their recoil – the backward movement caused by the firing of the shell – became more violent, the next step was to develop hydraulic buffers which could absorb some of this movement and reduce the shock of recoil.

## First of the 20th century guns

In 1897 the French, in great secrecy, introduced a new 75mm (3 in) gun which brought all these principles together. It was a light field gun, with a recoil brake, a shield to protect the gunners (since they could now stay close to the gun), a fast-operating breech mechanism, and a one-piece round of ammunition which used a brass cartridge with the shell attached, so that it could be loaded very quickly. This "quick-firer" revolutionized artillery overnight.

## The World Wars

The First World War (1914-1918) was fought with immense quantities of artillery, and many new types were evolved. Railway guns, anti-aircraft guns, heavy howitzers, and special light guns to be fired against tanks all appeared during the course of this war.

The Second World War (1939-45) brought more new ideas. Self-propelled guns were developed so that artillery could move alongside tanks and drive closer to their targets. Anti-tank guns became much more powerful in order to defeat thicker armored tanks. Anti-aircraft guns became bigger so that they could reach up to great altitudes to defend against bombers, and at the same time small fast-firing guns had to be developed for protection against ground attack aircraft.

Recoilless guns were invented for use where firepower without excessive weight was needed, as, for example, by parachute troops. New types of shells were developed for firing against different sorts of targets.

## Introduction of the missile

The Second World War, which saw so much inventiveness in the use of artillery, also saw the beginning of the weapon which was to replace artillery in many areas – the guided missile. Rockets were first used in war in the 18th century, but they were erratic and unreliable. But German development of the rocket in the period 1931-45, led to the V-1 and V-2 missiles, and to many other designs which were never manufactured. After the war the major nations all began research into missiles, using the German work as their starting point. Allied to this development was the perfection of the atomic bomb and later the hydrogen bomb. Within a few years atomic warheads for missiles and atomic shells for artillery were developed and tested. Add the electronic developments which led to the computer and the microchip, and the picture of modern artillery is complete.

**75mm Gun Modele** *(1897, France)*
This is the famous "French 75" which entered service in 1897 and remained in use until after the Second World War. It is of importance in the development of artillery since it was the first field gun to have a hydro-pneumatic on-carriage recoil system, a shield, to use a fixed round of ammunition and to have a quick-acting breech. It was the first of the famous "quick-firing" field guns. The Model 1897 was the principal French field artillery gun prior to World War One, since its rapid-fire characteristic fitted in well with the French tactical policy; it was not until the war settled into a siege that the French realized the need for heavier weapons, but even then the M1897 remained their standard divisional artillery piece.

**18-pounder Gun** *(1904, Britain)*
This gun was introduced into British service in 1904, in the aftermath of the South African War. It became the backbone of British divisional artillery during the First World War and, with periodic improvements, was to remain in British service until the end of the Second World War in 1945. The gun used a screw breech mechanism with fixed rounds of ammunition. The standard projectile was a shrapnel shell but this was later augmented by high explosive, smoke and (during World War One) gas shells.

**12-inch Howitzer** *(1917, Britain)*
This is included as an example of the super-heavy artillery developed during World War One for the purpose of smashing down the German defensive line. Because of its size it had to be transported in six loads, each towed by a caterpillar tractor, and when assembled it had 20.3 tonnes (20 tons) of soil shoveled into a box at the front of the carriage to prevent it tipping backwards when fired. The ammunition was separate loading, using an 11-part bagged charge, and high explosive shells were standard.

18-pounder gun

**155mm Gun GPF Mle** *(1917, France)*
The GPF (Grand Puissance, Filloux – High power, designed by Captain Filloux), was one of the weapons developed to provide heavier support than the 75mm M1897 could give the French Army in 1917. As might be expected of a weapon designed in wartime it was of simple pattern, robust and powerful. The ammunition was separate loading with a bagged charge and a high explosive shell was standard. The barrel and recoil system were removed from some field carriages and used to equip the first American 155mm self-propelled guns (the M12) in 1942. The Americans also developed smoke, illuminating, armor-piercing and gas shells for it.

**75mm Pack Howitzer M8/M116** *(1920s, USA)*
This was developed in the 1920s as a pack artillery weapon, and could be dismantled into seven pack loads for mule transport. The howitzer had a horizontal sliding breech block. The ammunition was semi-fixed, the cartridge and shell being supplied separately and fitted together to be loaded as one unit. The brass cartridge case held a four-part charge. Standard projectiles included high explosive and smoke, and there was a shaped charge anti-tank shell which, since the charge was not adjustable, was a fixed round. It was used by mountain troops and airborne formations, since it could be parachute-dropped in parts.

155mm gun GPF Mle

### Sexton Self-propelled 25-pounder Gun *(1940s, Britain)*

The British Army pioneered self-propelled guns in the 1920s, but abandoned them for various organizational reasons. In World War Two they developed a 25-pounder gun mounted on the chassis of the Canadian "Ram" tank, with an open-topped armored body carrying the gun, 105 rounds of ammunition and a crew of six. It was widely used by British and Commonwealth armies from 1943 until the late 1950s. The gun fired the same range of ammunition as the towed 25-pounder and had the same performance.

### 88mm Anti-Aircraft Guns Models 18, 36 and 41 *(1920s, Germany)*

This group of guns became collectively known as the "Eighty-Eight" during the Second World War, when they achieved a great deal of fame principally as anti-tank guns though they were originally designed as anti-aircraft weapons.

The design was done by Krupp technicians working in Sweden in the 1920s, and the first guns were built for the German Air Force in 1933. These were the "88mm Flak 18" models, "Flak" being an abbreviation for "Flieger Abwehr Kanone" or aircraft attack gun. The gun was a high velocity weapon with a semi-automatic sliding breech block which opened automatically after firing to throw out the empty case and closed automatically once the next round had been loaded.

After some experience it was decided to make a few improvements. The carriage was redesigned and the gun was built with the barrel lining in three pieces. Improved sights were fitted and this model became the Flak 36. During the Second World War, a third model was developed in order to give greater vertical range. This became known as the Flak 41. All three models were pressed into service as anti-tank guns from time to time, and they were exceedingly powerful and successful in this role. Some are still used by the defense forces of Spain and Yugoslavia as coastal defense weapons.

### 40mm Bofors Light Anti-Aircraft Gun *(1929, Sweden)*

One of the most famous guns in history, the 40mm Bofors has been used by almost every army in the world at some time or another since its inception in Sweden in 1929. The Bofors uses an automatic sliding breech block which is operated by the recoil of the gun. With a constant supply of ammunition, the earlier L/60 could fire at 120 rounds per minute, while the later L/70 fires at approximately 240 per minute. The L/60 was a hand-operated model, though the later models could be provided with radar data. The L/70 has full power operation and optical sights, and can also be fitted with the BOF1 fire control unit which incorporates a laser rangefinder and an electronic computer to aid in the aiming.

### 105mm light Field Howitzer Model 18 *(1929-30, Germany)*

The 105mm leFH18 was developed by Rheinmettal in 1929/1930 and entered German service in 1935 to become the standard equipment of the divisional artillery. The ammunition was of the separate loading type using a cartridge case which could be of either brass or steel. High explosive, smoke, illuminating and anti-tank shells could all be fired from it.

In 1940 the gun was fitted with a muzzle brake to reduce recoil, the recoil system was strengthened, and a long range shell and cartridge issued. This modified model of the 105mm then became known as the leFH18M. The next improvement demanded by the German Army was that the weight should be reduced, and to do this the gun and recoil system of the 18M was fitted to the carriage of the 75mm anti-tank gun PAK40.

### 8-inch Howitzer M1/M115 *(1930s, USA)*

The 8-inch howitzer was designed in the 1930s as a "partner piece" to the 155mm gun, which was a howitzer sharing the same design of carriage. The two barrels could be interchanged, though certain adjustments had to be made to them. Used by both the British and US armies until the 1950s, it has also been mounted on self-propelled carriages and in this form is still in use by both the US and British armies and many others.

**88mm anti-aircraft guns 18/36**

**40mm Bofors light anti-aircraft gun**

3.7-inch anti-aircraft gun

### 3.7-inch Anti-Aircraft Gun
*(1930s, Britain)*
This was designed in the 1930s, and was the principal British air defense gun of the Second World War. It was first issued in 1938 and it remained in service until the middle of·the 1950s. The 3.7-inch was an advanced gun for its time, being designed to be used with fire control predictors which were fed with information from range and height finders (later from radar) which signaled the elevation and direction to dials on the gun. The gunlayer merely had to move the gun until it matched the information on the dials and begin firing. There were no sights on the gun. The ammunition was a fixed round using a brass cartridge and a high explosive shell fitted with a time fuse or, later, a radio proximity fuse.

### 25-pounder Field Gun
*(1930s, Britain)*
This was developed in the early 1930s to replace the 18-pounder gun, and was designed in 87mm (3.45 in) caliber so that the barrel could be inserted into the carriage of the old 18-pounders. The design of a new carriage was begun in 1938. The British Army took the 18/25-pounder to France in 1939, and the all-new equipment was first used in Norway in 1940. It was later fitted with a muzzle brake to reduce the recoil when firing anti-tank shot. The ammunition was separate loading,

using a brass cartridge containing a three-part charge. High explosive, smoke, incendiary, flare and illuminating shells were provided, as well as a steel anti-tank shot. The 25-pounder was widely exported and is still in use in South Africa, Portugal, India and Pakistan.

### 105mm Howitzer M1/M101
*(1930s, USA)*
This was designed in the early 1930s and was issued in 1940 to become the US Army's standard divisional artillery piece. It was originally known as the M1, and was redesignated M101 after the Second World War. The gun is of conventional type, with a horizontal sliding breech block. In addition to being used in towed equipments, the gun has been fitted to a number of self-propelled systems.

105mm howitzer M101

### 155mm Gun M1/M59 *(1930s, USA)*
This was another weapon developed in the late 1930s, in this case to replace the 155mm GPF (see p. 34) which had been adopted from the French in 1917. The new design was far more powerful and was mounted on a carriage which, for its day, was almost revolutionary. It was a split-trail pattern with a bogie carrying four dual wheels under the front end of the carriage and a two-wheeled limber. Ammunition was separate loading, using a two-part bag charge. The standard shell was a high explosive type, but armor-piercing and smoke were also provided. The armor-piercing shell was actually intended for use in the anti-ship role in coast defense, but it occasionally proved useful in the anti-tank role. The gun was originally known as the M1, but in the 1950s was redesignated the M59. It was used by both the US and British armies; neither use it now.

### 155mm Howitzer M1/M114
*(1930s, USA)*
This was developed in the late 1930s as the M1 howitzer, replacing the M1917 design which had been purchased from France during the course of the First World War. Ammunition of the 155mm howitzer is separate loading, using bagged charges. The projectiles provided include high explosive, illuminating, smoke, anti-personnel sub-munitions, and nuclear munitions.

### 150mm heavy Field Howitzer Model 18 *(1935, Germany)*

This was the standard German Army medium support howitzer, and it stayed in service from 1935 to 1945. The gun was conventional, with a sliding breech block and used separate loading cased charges to fire a variety of HE, smoke and anti-tank projectiles. The carriage was a two-wheeled split trail pattern. This weapon deserves mention as being the first to use a rocket-assisted shell to increase the range. This was issued in 1941 and saw some use on the Eastern Front, but proved to be too complicated and not very accurate and so was withdrawn after a short trial period. Eventually a number of guns had muzzle brakes fitted to reduce the recoil and allow more powerful charges; these became known as "Model 18."

### 152mm Gun-Howitzer M37 *(1936, Russia)*

This entered Soviet service in 1936 as a replacement for an earlier design, though in fact the earlier weapon lingered until the 1960s. The gun has a large multiple-baffle muzzle brake and a screw breech mechanism, firing separate loading cased charge ammunition. The carriage is a twin dual wheel split trail type with two prominent balancing spring cases in front of the shield. Projectiles available for the gun-howitzer include high explosive, concrete-piercing, armor-piercing, chemical, smoke, illuminating, and anti-tank.

### 122mm Howitzer M1938 *(1938, Russia)*

This was developed in 1938 for the Soviet Army and must be one of the most widely distributed guns of all time, since it is now in use in almost every African, Middle and Far Eastern state, Cuba, Indonesia and Yugoslavia, as well as being still in first-line service throughout the Warsaw Pact countries.

The howitzer is of conventional design, with a screw breech and a recoil system which is divided, the buffer beneath the gun and the recuperator above it. The carriage is a two-wheeled split trail type with box girder trail legs and a shield. Ammunition is of the separate loading type, using a brass or steel cartridge case, and projectiles available run the full range of high explosive, smoke and chemical types.

### 5.5-inch Medium Gun *(1930s, Britain)*

This was designed in the late 1930s to replace the existing 150mm (6 in) guns and howitzers that were of World War One vintage. It had an unusual quick-release on the elevating mechanism so that the gunlayer could continue laying the gun while the barrel was disconnected from the sights and swung down to a convenient angle for loading. Ammunition was of separate loading bagged charge type and high explosive shell was the standard. The first shells issued weighed 45kg (99 lbs).

122mm howitzer M1938

### 75mm Anti-tank gun Model 40 *(1940, Germany)*

This was the principal German anti-tank gun from 1940 to 1945; although it was not so powerful as the 88mm models, it was quite sufficient to deal with most British and American tanks of their time. The gun used a muzzle brake and was fitted with a semi-automatic sliding breech block mechanism. Ammunition was of the cased fixed type, and high explosive, armor-piercing shot and shaped-charge shells were provided. The carriage was a two-wheeled split trail type with shield, with a very low silhouette allowing it to be concealed very easily.

152mm gun-howitzer M37

75mm anti-tank gun M40

88mm anti-tank gun M43

### 210mm Railway Gun Model 12
*(1939, Germany)*
This is included as an example of the long range railway guns which were once common among continental armies, and also as an example of specialized super-long range gun design. The Kanone 12(E) (E for "Eisenbahn") was intended to be the Second World War equal of the First World War's "Paris Gun," a long range gun which bombarded Paris from a range of 113km (70 miles). This demanded enormous power, and since a conventional copper driving band could not stand the stress, the gun was rifled with eight deep grooves and the shell made with eight curved ribs. When loading, the ribs had to be fitted carefully into the grooves, and their action gave the shell the necessary spin. The charge was enormous; 241kg (531 lbs) of powder divided into three bags, the final bag in a steel case.

### 76mm Divisional Gun M1942
**(ZIS-3)** *(1942, Russia)*
This was introduced in 1942 and was the last in a long series of 76mm Russian designs. It uses a two-wheeled split-trail carriage with tubular trail legs, and the gun is carried in a divided recoil system based on that of the German 105mm leFH18. The barrel has a muzzle brake and a vertical sliding semi- automatic breech block , and it uses a fixed round of ammunition.

High explosive, smoke and anti-tank projectiles were all provided. Although no longer in first-line service with any Warsaw Pact army, it is still held in their reserve forces and has been widely exported; it can be found in almost every African and Middle Eastern country.

### 105mm light Field Howitzer Model 43 *(1943, Germany)*
After some experience on the Eastern Front, the German Army asked for a field weapon which could fire at high angles, so that it could be concealed in forests and fire through the trees. The leFH43 was conventional, a 105mm weapon with muzzle brake and sliding breech block, though the barrel was longer and the chamber larger than those of the leFH18. Unfortunately the design and development process took so long that the war ended before it was completed.

### 88mm Anti-tank Gun Model 43
*(1943, Germany)*
When the 88mm Flak 41 gun was developed it was decided to make a proper anti-tank gun in the same caliber; anti-aircraft guns are generally too cumbersome for the anti-tank task and are difficult to hide. Krupp therefore designed the 88mm PAK (Panzer Abwehr Kanone – tank attack gun) Model 43. The gun was completely new, using a different cartridge to the air defense guns, and

122mm field gun D-74

could send an armor-piercing shot at over 1100 metres (3610 ft) per second to penetrate 184mm (7.5 in) of armor at 2000m (6560 ft) range, a terrifying performance.
In 1943 the war in Russia demanded more anti-tank guns, and while the guns could be made more quickly, the carriages for the PAK43 took more time. As an emergency measure the PAK 43/41 was devised; this used the PAK43 gun on a two-wheeled split-trail carriage put together from existing parts – the wheels from the 150mm howitzer, trail legs from the 105mm howitzer and so on – and did terrible execution on the Eastern Front.

### 122mm Field Gun D-74
*(1955, Russia)*
This appeared in 1955 as a replacement for an earlier design but has not been made in large numbers. The D-74 gun uses a muzzle brake and has a semi-automatic vertical sliding breech block mechanism. The carriage is a two-wheeled split trail. Ammunition is separate loading, and high explosive, chemical, smoke, illuminating and armor-piercing projectiles are available.

### 130mm Field Gun M46
*(1950s, Russia)*

This was developed at the same time as the 122mm D-74 and was selected for service in the Warsaw Pact armies because it offered a better combination of shell weight and performance. It was derived from an existing 130mm (5 in) naval gun and uses a muzzle brake and horizontal sliding breech block.

### OTO-Melara 105mm Model 56 Pack Howitzer *(1950s, Italy)*

This went into production in 1957, and has been adopted by over 25 countries. As a pack howitzer, it is capable of being dismantled into 11 component parts for transporting. The carriage is a split-trail type, the trail legs being hinged and jointed and the wheels mounted on eccentric axles so that the gun can be set high when firing as a howitzer or set low to the ground for anti-tank firing. The barrel is fitted with a muzzle brake and uses a vertical sliding breech block in which the block rises to open. The ammunition used is the same as that of the American M1/M101.

### Abbot 105mm Self-propelled Gun
*(1950s, Britain)*

Abbot was developed in the late 1950s as a replacement for the Sexton SP gun. The gun is fitted with a muzzle brake and fume extractor and is in a turret which can revolve through 360° to permit firing in any direction. The vehicle is based on the same chassis and components as the

105mm M56 pack howitzer

FV432 Armored Personnel Carrier; the driver is at the front, with the engine at his right, and the turret on top. The gun is manned by a three-man crew – commander, gunlayer, and loader – and there is a power-operated rammer to load the shell, the cartridge being loaded by hand. Abbot is in service with the British and Indian armies. It is expected that it will be replaced in British service by a new 155mm self-propelled howitzer, the SP-70, in the late 1980s.

### 155mm Bofors Howitzer FH-77
*(1960s, Sweden)*

This design was the result of studies by the Swedish Army in the 1960s and was the first 155mm howitzer with auxiliary propulsion to be manufactured. A Volvo engine drives hydraulic pumps which provide power for the wheels, elevating and traversing the gun, lifting and

lowering the trail wheels, opening the trail legs and ramming the shell. The gun is fitted with a muzzle brake and has a sliding breech block. Ammunition is separate loading, using a plastic-cased charge.

### 122mm Howitzer D-30
*(1960s, Russia)*

This is the latest of a long series of 122mm howitzers used by the Russians from the turn of the century. The carriage is two-wheeled, with three trail legs that fold together. The gun is rotated 180° and clamped to the trail legs, and the towing attachment is part of the muzzle brake. In action the three legs are spread out at 120° spacing and the wheels raised from the ground, giving the gun a full 360° of traverse. It can elevate to 70° for high angle fire if required.

Abbot 105mm SP gun

122mm howitzer D-30

155mm SP howitzer M109

155mm howitzer M198

### 155mm Self-propelled Howitzer M109 *(1963, USA)*

The US Army developed two self-propelled 155mm howitzers during, and shortly after, the Second World War, but both were open-topped. In the late 1950s it was decided to develop a new howitzer with full armor protection. The resulting self-propelled howitzer appeared in 1963 and was designated the M109.

The M109 is based on a tracked chassis specially developed for the purpose, and is constructed of aluminum armor. The gun is carried in a turret capable of revolving through 360°. It is fitted with a muzzle brake and also with a fume extractor which prevents powder smoke from flowing into the turret when the breech is opened after firing.

### 105mm Howitzer M102 *(1964, USA)*

This was designed to replace the M101 in certain artillery units where a lighter gun was advantageous – eg, those in the Allied Mobile Force and Rapid Deployment Force whose guns were normally helicopter-lifted, and in Airborne and Air-Mobile divisions. The first guns were issued in 1964 and were used in combat in Vietnam. The gun is rather longer than the M1/M101 type and has a vertical sliding breech block.

The ammunition used with the M102 is the same as that used with the M1/M101 howitzer, but the longer barrel gives a slightly better performance.

### 105mm Light Gun L118A1 *(1974, Britain)*

In 1965 the British Army requested a replacement for the OTO-Melara M56 and the Light Gun was the result. The Light Gun uses an unusual tubular trail which widens so that two gunners can stand inside it to operate the breech and load. The gun is fitted with a muzzle brake and a vertical sliding breech block and is electrically fired. It uses separate loading cased-charge ammunition, of the same type as that used in the "Abbot" self-propelled gun. A circular firing platform is carried on the trail; in action, this is placed on the ground and the gun's wheels run on to it so that for wide changes of direction the wheels run around the smooth surface of the platform. For traveling the gun is swung completely round and the barrel locked to the trail.

### 155mm howitzer G5

### 155mm Howitzer G5 *(1976, South Africa)*

Development of this gun began in 1976 after various foreign guns were examined and tested. The gun is fitted with a muzzle brake and uses a screw breech similar to that of the American M109 howitzer. It fires a bagged charge separate loading round and the shells are of the "ERFB" (Extended Range, Full Bore) type.

### 155mm Howitzer M198 *(1978, USA)*

This weapon was developed in the late 1960s as a replacement for the 155mm howitzer M1/M114 Model. The projectiles are of a new design family and include high explosive, illuminating, rocket-assisted explosive, carrier shell containing anti-tank mines, carrier shell containing anti-personnel bomblets, and nuclear.

155mm FH-70 howitzer

175mm SP gun M107

### 155mm FH-70 Howitzer
*(1978, Britain, West Germany and USA)*
In the early 1960s Britain, West Germany and the USA agreed to develop a 155mm howitzer which they would all use. Eventually the USA went its own way and developed the M198 and Italy joined with Britain and Germany to develop the FH-70. Britain was responsible for the carriage, high explosive shell and cartridge; Germany developed the gun, loading system, auxiliary propulsion unit (APU) and sights; Italy the cradle, recoil system and some ammunition components.

The FH-70 has a split trail carriage with an APU at the front end. This consists of a gasoline engine which drives the main gun wheels so that the weapon can be moved without requiring a tractor. The gun is fitted with a muzzle brake.

### 175mm Self-propelled Gun M107
*(1962, USA)*
The 175mm gun was developed in the late 1950s with the intention of producing a heavy gun which would be light enough to be air portable. Production first commenced in 1962 , and continued through until 1980. The M107 uses a tracked chassis developed for the purpose and later adopted to other SP equipments. The gun is of conventional design, using a screw breech with percussion firing mechanism. The ammunition is separate loading, using a three-part bagged charge. The only projectile provided is a high explosive type.

Behind the breech is a combined ammunition hoist and power rammer which lifts the shell from the rear or the left side of the vehicle, and rams it into the chamber.

### 155mm Self-propelled Gun GCT
*(1979, France)*
Development of this equipment began in 1969 and issues to the French Army started in 1979.
The commander supervises the work of the gunner and the loader. The loader can select, on a switchboard, the number and type of rounds to be fired. On pressing the "fire" button the automatic loading system selects the shell from the ammunition rack, carries it to the breech and rams it. The gunlayer, on the right side of the turret, has a computer-aided sight which receives data by radio link and displays it digitally.

155mm SP gun GCT

### 155mm Gun Modele TR
*(1982, France)*
The French developed a number of 155mm guns after the GPF, and the Modele TR is the latest in the series, having been developed in the late 1970s and approved for French Army use in 1982. It is similar to other designs of the same period, a split-trail carriage with an auxiliary power unit mounted in front of the main gun wheels, and with secondary wheels on the trail legs for steering. The gun is fitted with a muzzle brake and has a horizontal sliding breech block . The ammunition is separate loading with bagged charges and high explosive, smoke and illuminating shells are available. For traveling the gun is swung through 180° and clamped along the trail legs.

V1 missile (FZG-76)

MISSILES

### V-1 Missile (FZG-76)
*(1944, Germany)*
V-1 stands for "Vergeltungswaffen 1" – Vengeance Weapon 1. It was the first missile of any sort used in war, though it was unguided and was, in fact, a pilotless airplane. It consisted of an airframe with wings and tail, propelled by a ramjet motor above the body, and with the nose packed with 850kg (1874 lbs) of high explosive. It was launched from a ramp by a piston which gave it sufficient speed to allow the ramjet motor to take over and propel it at about 600km/hr (373 mph). The first one was fired against London in 1944, and they continued unabated until March 1945.

### A-4 Rocket (V-2) *(1944, Germany)*
Vengeance Weapon 2 was known to the Germans as "Aggregate 4" a cover name. It was a fin-stabilized rocket developed from 1934 onwards through a series of gradually improved designs, until the A-4 was perfected in 1944. The rocket motor was a single-stage liquid-fueled type, and the missile was launched vertically and then turned on to a predetermined course, using pre-

programmed controls to position it and then to shut off the flow of fuel so that it would complete its flight, on a ballistic trajectory. The warhead contained 1.016 tonne (1 ton) of Amatol high explosive and a simple impact fuse which allowed the warhead to bury itself in the ground before detonating.
Production of the A-4 began early in 1944 and it was first fired against England on September 8 of that year. In all, about 10,000 were produced, of which 1115 were fired against England, and 1341 against Antwerp.

### Wasserfall Air Defense Missile
*(1942, Germany)*
This was the world's first air defense guided missile, designed in 1942, to destroy aircraft at altitudes up to 20,000m (65,000 ft), at speeds up to 900km/hr (560 mph) and at ranges up to 50km (31 miles) from the launching site. It was a liquid-fueled rocket with radio guidance, and the 235kg (518 lbs) warhead was to be fitted with a proximity fuse which would detonate within lethal distance of a target. The first rocket flew in 1944 but the program was stopped in 1945.

### SA-2 "Guideline" Air Defense Missile *(1950s, Russia)*
Guideline is probably the most widely used air defense missile in the world, since the Soviets have exported it to many countries. The missile is a fin-stabilized rocket attached to a boost motor which also carries fins. The boost motor uses solid propellant and burns for about 4 seconds, after which the liquid-fuel main rocket takes over and burns for another 22 seconds. A radar tracks the target and a computer steers the missile into the radar beam, and keeps it there by means of radio controls. The missile warhead is 130kg (286 lbs) of explosive inside a serrated steel casing, operated by a proximity fuse. There have been several improvements to Guideline including better radars, better fuses and different types of warhead.

### Rapier Air Defense Missile
*(1950s, Britain)*
The original Rapier relies on an optical sight. The launcher unit carries four missiles and contains a surveillance radar set. The operator slews the launcher in the target's direction and uses the optical sight to track it. He then fires a missile, keeping the sight on the target. The missile is "gathered" into the sight line. Any difference between flight line and sight line is corrected by radio.

### Missile System MGM-5A (Corporal)
*(1952, USA)*
Corporal was the first tactical missile to be developed after the Second World War and owed a great deal to the German research scientists who had worked at the research station at Peenemunde. Indeed, in many respects Corporal was no more than an improved V-2. It used liquid propellant and adopted a ballistic trajectory after the fuel had been shut off by radio command. But it needed an enormous technological retinue. It was issued to troops in 1953, and it was the first weapon to place the nuclear warhead into the control of troops in the field.

### MGM-5A Corporal

Milan anti-tank missile

Swingfire anti-tank missile

### Missile System MIM-14A (Nike Hercules) *(1953, USA)*

The Nike family of air defense missiles began in the immediate postwar years and the first Nike missile site was operational in the USA in 1953. This became known as "Nike Ajax" and was a somewhat cumbersome system which used two radar beams, one to track the target and the other to control the flight of the missile.

In 1958 Nike Hercules was adopted to replace Ajax. The new missile was 15 times more effective than Ajax. The warhead could be high explosive fragmentation or nuclear, and the Hercules had a secondary role as an interceptor of incoming missiles, the ability of which was proved several times in tests. It is believed that a few batteries remain in service, as the replacement for the Hercules, the Patriot missile, has not as yet been fully entered into service.

### Blowpipe Air Defense Missile
*(1960s, Britain)*

Blowpipe was developed privately by Short Brothers in the mid-1960s and then adopted by the British Army. It is one of the few western air defense missiles which has been proved in combat, in the Falklands campaign. An ejection motor launches the missile at low velocity, after which the main thrust motor accelerates it to a speed of mach 1.5. Guidance is done by the operator using a joystick and commands are sent to the missile by radio. A radio proximity fuse detonates the warhead.

### Milan Anti-tank Missile
*(1960s, France and Germany)*

Milan means "Missile Infanterie Legere, Anti-Char" – Light infantry anti-tank missile – and was developed by Aerospatiale of France and Messerschmitt-Bolkow-Blohm of Germany in the 1960s.

Milan consists of a rocket with shaped-charge warhead, sealed into a launch tube. This is clipped to the "Launcher Post," a tripod and sight unit, and the operator takes aim at a tank. The rocket accelerates to the target, unreeling a fine control wire as it goes. In the tail is an infrared flare, and this is detected by a sensor in the sight unit; the operator keeps his sight lined up on the target and the sensor measures the difference between the sight line and the flight of the missile, calculates corrections, and signals them down the wire to steer the rocket into alignment with the sight.

### FROG-7 Battlefield Tactical Rocket
*(1967, Russia)*

FROG is a NATO term meaning "Free Flight Rocket, Over Ground." FROG-7, which appeared in 1967, is a solid-fuel rocket, fin stabilized, fired from a simple rail carried on an eight-wheeled launcher. FROG-7 has a standard high explosive warhead containing about 450kg (993 lbs) of TNT or a nuclear warhead believed to be of about 3-5kt yield. FROG-7 has been supplied widely to Middle and Far Eastern countries, with the standard warhead.

### Swingfire Anti-tank Missile
*(1969, Britain)*

The British Army began backing the development of an anti-tank missile in the late 1950s, but their first venture collapsed. The remains of the project was taken over by Vickers and from it they developed the Swingfire missile which went into service in 1969. It is wire-guided and controlled by joystick by the operator. The warhead is a shaped charge which is capable of defeating almost any tank in existence head-on. It is normally mounted in the "Striker" tracked vehicle, which carries five missiles ready to launch and five to re-load.

### FROG-7 battlefield Tactical Rocket

## Missile System BGM-71A (TOW)
*(1970, USA)*

TOW stands for "Tube launched, Optically tracked, Wire guided." It is the US Army's standard anti-tank missile which can be fired from a tripod, from armored vehicles or from helicopters. The missile consists of solid fuel booster and sustainer motors, a shaped charge warhead, and control actuators which move the wings when commanded by instructions passed down a trailing wire. Operation is by the firer keeping the sight on the target, while an infrared sensor in the sight detects a flare in the missile tail and then develops commands to bring sight line and flight line into agreement.

## Missile System MGM-52A (Lance)
*(1972, USA)*

Developed in the 1960s, this missile entered American service in 1972. It was later adopted by Britain, West Germany, Israel, Belgium, Italy and the Netherlands and is still in service with all these armies.

Lance is a liquid propellant rocket which is carried on and launched from a small tracked carrier; each carrier is supported by a second vehicle with two reloads. There is also a special lightweight launch vehicle which can be helicopter-lifted or parachute-dropped. Guidance is inertial, the missile computer being programmed with launch location and target location during the preparation phase. Warheads include high explosive, nuclear (10 kiloton yield), enhanced radiation (the "neutron" warhead) and a number of multiple sub-munition designs that contain various smaller warheads which are released over the target.

## SA-8 "Gecko" Air Defense Missile
*(1975, Russia)*

Gecko is among the latest Soviet missiles, first seen in 1975. It is self-contained, being carried on a six-wheeled amphibious chassis. On this is the launch unit with four missiles and a surveillance radar. In front of this unit is the "guidance

MGM-52A Lance

group" consisting of a tracking radar, two missile guidance beam radars, an optical tracker and a television tracker. The two guidance radars suggest that it is capable of firing two missiles at once and controlling them independently, and the design of the radar antenna suggest that the radar operates on the "agile frequency" principle, shifting frequency several times a second to avoid electronic countermeasures.

## Roland Air Defense Missile *(1977, France and West Germany)*

Roland is yet another combined development by Aerospatiale of France and MBB of Germany. It was originally a "fair-weather" system, using a radar to detect the target and then an optical sight to track it and control the engagement. The target is acquired by either the radar or the optical sight. The sight or tracking radar is locked to the target, and the missile is detected either by radar or by an infrared flare in its tail.

## HOT Anti-tank Missile
*(1977, France)*

HOT means "Haut-Subsonique Optiquement Teleguide Tire d'un Tube" – High-subsonic, wire-guided, fired from a tube – and is the larger partner of Milan, having been developed by the same two companies. It is a rocket with shaped-

charge warhead pre-loaded and sealed into a launch tube. Unlike Milan, HOT is some distance from its operator and probably divided from him by armor, so there is no need to launch at low speed, and it leaves its launcher at high velocity to give an average speed of about 1000km/hr (620mph). The warhead is extremely powerful and can pierce over 1m (3.3 ft) of armor plate, greater than found on any tank.

## Missile System FIM-92A (Stinger)
*(1980, USA)*

Stinger is a shoulder-fired air defense missile which entered service in 1980. It is placed on the operator's shoulder and aimed at the target through a simple optical sight. The operator then presses a button which sends an interrogatory signal and checks whether the target is enemy. If it is, a tone is sounded and the operator presses the trigger. This starts the control gyroscope and super-cools the infrared seeker which then begins to operate. As soon as it has detected and locked on to the target the missile launches itself. It is locked to the exhaust emission of the target aircraft, but it strikes the aircraft and not the hot gases behind it.

# Missiles and Artillery in Service Today

| Country | Close Support Artillery | Medium Support Artillery | Battlefield Missiles and Rockets | Anti-tank Weapons | Air Defence Weapons |
|---|---|---|---|---|---|
| Argentina | 105H leFH18, 105 Pack M56; 105H M101 | 155G M59; 155H M114; 155G F3 | 105RL | 106RCL; SS-11 GW; SS-12 GW; Bantam GW | 40 Bofors; 90G M117; Roland |
| Belgium | 105 Pack M56; 105H M101; 105H M102; 105SPH M108 | 155G M59; 155H M114; 155SPH M44; 155SPH M109; 203SPH M115; 203SPH M110 | Lance | Swingfire GW; Milan GW | 40 Bofors; 57 Bofors; Hawk; Nike |
| Brazil | 75H M8; 105H M101; 105H M102; 105 Pack M56 | 155H M114 | 108RL | 106RCL; Cobra GW | 35 Oerlikon; 40 Bofors; 90G M117; Roland |
| Canada | 105 Pack M56; 105H M101 | 155SPH M109 | | 106RCL; TOW GW | 40 Bofors; Blowpipe |
| China | 100G; 122H | 122G; 130G; M46; 152H | 320RL | 57G; 76G; Sagger GW | 57G; 85G; 100G |
| Egypt | 85G D-44; 100G M-1944 | 122G M1937; 122H D-74; 130G M46; 152H M37; 180G S-23 | FROG-7; Samlet GW; Scud GW | Sagger GW; Snapper GW; Swingfire GW; Milan GW; HOT GW; | 37G; 40 Bofors; 57G; 85G; Guideline GW; Goa GW; Gainful GW; |
| France | 105 Pack M56; 105H M101 | 155H F3; 155H TR; 155SPH GCT | Pluton | 106RCL; Milan GW; SS-11 GW; HOT GW; Harpon GW; Entac GW | 30G; 40 Bofors; Roland |
| Germany (West) | 105 Pack M56; 105H M101 | 155H M114; 155H FH-70; 155SPH M109; 175SPG M107 | 110RL; Lance; Pershing | 106RCL; HOT GW; Milan GW; TOW GW | 35 Oerlikon; 40 Bofors; Roland; Hawk; Redeye; Nike |
| Iran | 75 Pack M8; 85G D-44; 105H M101 | 130G M46; 155SPH M109; 155H M114; 175SPG M107; 203H M115; 203SPH M110; | 122RL | 106RCL; TOW GW; Dragon GW; SS-11 GW | 40 Bofors; 57G; 85G; Hawk; Rapier; Tigercat; Strela |
| Iraq | 105 Pack M56; 85G D-44 | 122H M1937; 122H M1938; 130G M46; 152H M1937; 155SPH GCT | 122RL; FROG; Scud | 85G; HOT GW; TOW GW; Sagger GW; Milan GW | 37G; 57G; 85G; Guideline; Goa; Gainful; Strela; Gaskin |
| Israel | 105H M101; 105SPH M107; 122G D-30 | 122H M1938; 130G M46; 155H M144; 155SPH M109; 175SPG M107 | 160RL; 240RL; Lance | 106RCL; Sagger; TOW GW; Dragon GW | 20 Oerlikon; 40 Bofors; Redeye; Chaparral; Hawk |
| Italy | 105 Pack M56; 105H M101 | 155H M114; 155SPH M44; 155G M59; 155SPH M109 | Lance; Firos-25 RL | 106RCL; Cobra GW; TOW GW | 40 Bofors; Hawk; Nike |
| Japan | 75 Pack M8; 105H M101; 105SPH M52 | 155SPH Type 75; 155SPH M44; 155H M114; 155G M59; 203H M115; 203SPH M110 | 130RL; 300RL | 106RCL; Type 64 GW; KAM-3D GW | 35 Oerlikon; 40 Bofors; 90G; Redeye; Hawk; Nike |
| Libya | 105H M101 | 122SPH M74; 122G D-30; 122H D-74; 130G M46; 152H D-20; 155H M114; 155SOH M109 | 107RL; 122RL; 130RL | Vigilant GW; Sagger GW | 40 Bofors; 57G; Crotale; Guideline; Goa; Gainful; Strela; Gaskin |
| Netherlands | 105H M101; 105SPH AMX-61 | 155H M114; 155H M198; 155SPH M109; 175SPG M107; 203SPH M110 | Lance | 106RCL; TOW GW | 40 Bofors; Hawk; Nike |
| Saudi Arabia | 105H M101; 105H M102 | 155H M114; 155H FH-70; 155SPH GCT; 155SPH M109; 203SPH M110 | | SS-11 GW; Harpon GW; TOW GW; Dragon GW | 20 Oerlikon; 30 Oerikon; Hawk; Shahine; Redeye |
| South Africa | 25-pr G | 5.5in G; 155H G5 | 127 Valkiri RL | 6-pr G; 17-pr G; Entac GW | 20 Oerlikon; 35 Oerlikon; 40 Bofors; 3.7in G; Crotale; Tigercat |
| Spain | 105 Pack M56; 105SPH M52; 105SPH M108 | 155H M114; 155SPH M109; 155SPH M44; 175SPG M107; 203H M115; 203SPH M110 | 216RL; 306RL; 380RL | 106RCL; Milan GW; Dragon GW; TOW GW | 20 Oerlikon; 35 Oerlikon; 40 Bofors; Hawk; Nike |
| Sweden | 105H M4140 | 155SPH Bandkanon; 155H Mle 50; 150H M39; 155H FH-77 | | 90RCL; Bantam GW, TOW GW; BILL | 120 Oerlikon; 40 Bofors; Redeye; Hawk; Bloodhound; RBS-70 |
| Syria | 85G D-44; 100G M1944 | 122H M-1938; 122H D-30; 130G M46; 152H D-1; 180G S-23 | FROG; Scud; 107RL; 140RL; 240RL | Sagger GW; Snapper GW; HOT GW; Milan GW | 37G; 57G; 85G; Guideline; Gainful; Strela; Gecko; Gaskin |
| Turkey | 75 Pack M8; 105H M101; 105SPH M7; 105SPH M108 | 155SPH M109; 155H M114; 155G M59; 175SPG M107; 203H M115; 203HSPH M110 | Honest John RL | 106RCL; SS-11 GW; TOW GW; Cobra GW; Milan GW | 40 Bofors; 90G; Nike |
| USSR (and Warsaw Pact) | 100SPG SU-100; 76 Mtn Gun; 85G D-44 | 122H D-30; 122H M1938; 122SPH M74; 130G M46; 152SPH M73; 152H D-1; 152H D-20; 180G S-23 | FROG; Scud; Scaleboard; 122RL; 140RL; 240RL; 250RL; SS-21; SS-22; SS-23 | 85G D-48; 100G T-12; Sagger GW; Swatter GW; Spiral GW; Spigot GW; Spandrel GW | 57G; Guild; Guideline; Goa; Ganef; Gammon; Gainful; Strela; Gecko; Gaskin; SA-10; SA-11; SA-12; SA-13; |
| United Kingdom | 105 Light G; 105SPH Abbot | 155SPH M109; 155H FH-70; 175SPG M107; 203SPH M110 | Lance; MLRS | SS-11 GW; Swingfire; Milan; TOW GW | Blowpipe; Rapier; Javelin |
| USA | 105H M101; 105H M102; 105SPH M108 | 155SPH M109; 155SPH M44; 155H M114; 155H M198 | Lance; Pershing; MLRS | 106RCL; TOW GW; Dragon GW | 20 Vulcan; Redeye GW; Stinger; Hawk; Nike; Chaparral; 40 Bofors SPG |

Notes on the Foregoing: Numbers represent calibre in millimetres, except for 6-pr, 17-pr, 25-pr guns and 3.7in and 5.5in guns.

Abbreviations:
| | | | | | | | |
|---|---|---|---|---|---|---|---|
| G | Gun | SPG | Self-propelled Gun | RCL | Recoilless Gun | GW | Guided Weapon |
| H | Howitzer | SPH | Self-propelled Howitzer | RL | Rocket Launcher | MLRS | Multiple Launch Rocket System |

# Glossary

**Area defense** Anti-aircraft and missile defenses designed to protect an area of ground, such as a city.

**Balancing gear** Spring or pneumatic cylinders which support the weight of the gun barrel so that the hand-wheel for elevation is easier to turn.

**Beam riding** Method of missile control in which the missile contains a radar receiver and control system which automatically keeps it in the center of a radar beam laid on the target.

**Breech mechanism** Mechanical arrangement for opening and closing a gun breech for loading; may be a sliding block or a cylindrical block with interrupted screw threads.

**Caliber** Internal diameter of a gun's barrel, measured from the surface between the rifling grooves.

**Cartridge** Explosive charge used in a gun to generate gas and thrust the projectile from the barrel and to the target.

**Command guidance** Method of guiding a missile by sending instructions to it during flight. Command guidance is accurate, but open to electronic interference.

**Driving band** Soft copper or plastic band on a projectile which engages in the gun's rifling and thus makes the shell spin.

**Electronic countermeasures** Methods used to protect a missile from electronic detection or electronically guided attack.

**Fire and forget** Missile in which the guidance is self-contained and requires no further instruction after firing, so that the operator can fire it, forget it and then go on to deal with another target.

**Firing platform** Round steel plate which is placed on the ground beneath the gun; the gun wheels run on to it. It allows the gun to be swung from side to side easily on the smooth surface of the platform.

**Fuse** The device which detonates the shell at the required moment: can be **impact**, operating when it hits; **delay**, operating shortly after it hits; **time**, operating in the air at some set time after firing; or **proximity**, operating when it detects the presence of a target. Fuses can be fitted to the nose or base of a shell or anywhere in a missile.

**Gun** Artillery piece which fires at high velocity, usually with a flat trajectory, ie with elevation less than 45°.

**HEAT (High Explosive Anti-Tank)** Projectile or warhead for the defeat of armor. HEAT uses a shaped charge of explosive.

**HESH (High Explosive Squash-Head)** Projectile used for defeat of armor. It contains plastic explosive which detonates outside the armor and shakes the inside surface of the tank loose.

**Homing** A system in which a missile flies to impact with its target by means of some self-contained system (radar, infrared, laser) which detects the target and steers the missile toward it.

**Howitzer** Artillery piece which fires at low velocity and with a high trajectory, ie with elevations which may be greater than 45°. Compared to a gun of the same caliber, a howitzer usually fires a heavier shell to less range.

**Inertial guidance** Method of guiding a missile using an artificial reference system inside the missile. The advantage is that the system is immune to outside interference.

**Infrared homing** An infrared detector within a missile is sensitive to heat which is given off by a target. As the missile detects the heat source, it homes in for attack.

**Laser homing** Electronic device that pin-points a target for the approach of a missile. The missile detects the reflection of the laser beam from the target and homes in on this.

**Mortar** Artillery piece which fires only at elevations above 45°. Modern mortars are usually smooth-bored and used by infantry.

**Point defense** Defense of a particularly vital area of ground, such as a factory.

**Predicted fire** Opening fire on a target without ranging, relying on having made corrections for weather and other conditions correctly.

**Primer** The device in the cartridge which ignites the propellant and fires the gun. May be **percussion**, operating when struck by a firing pin; or **electric**, requiring a current to go through it.

**Ranging** The process of adjusting the gun's fire to hit the target. Done by firing at an estimated range and then making corrections until the shot hits the target, after which all guns fire on the same data.

**Rifling** Helical grooves inside a gun barrel which spin the projectile and thus cause it to fly point-first.

**Shaped charge** A charge of high explosive formed with a hollowed-out face which is lined with metal. On detonating, the shape causes the effect to be "focused" so as to blast a hole through hard targets such as armor. Used in shells and missiles.

**Shell** Hollow projectile fired by artillery; may contain explosive, smoke composition or other agents.

**Shot** Solid projectile fired by artillery, usually for the defeat of armor.

**Soleplate** A plate of metal on the base of a gun or howitzer. It is lowered to the ground for firing to provide a stable base.

**Sub-munitions** The smaller bombs, mines or charges that are contained within a larger missile or shell, and are often dispensed over the target.

**Tracking** Automatically following a target by means of radar, optical or other sensors.

**Traveling clamp** Stay used to hold the gun barrel when traveling, so as to prevent strain being placed on the elevating gear. Sometimes called a **barrel clamp**.

**Velocity** The speed at which the shell travels: called **muzzle velocity** as it leaves the gun; **remaining velocity** at any other point in flight; and **terminal velocity** at the target.

# Index

A-4 Rocket (V-2) 42
Abbot 105mm Self-propelled Gun 39
ADATS (Air Defense Anti-Tank Systems) 31
air defense guns 8, 28
air defense missiles 10, 15, 18, 29
aircraft 12, 28
anti-tank missiles 8, 10, 11, 14, 15, 18, 32

ballistic missile 6
Blowpipe Air Defense Missile 18, 43
bomblet 30
breech block 7
BS-3 27

cartridges 7, 21, 24
Chapparal 29
chemicals 24
coastal defense gun 17
compass bearings 6, 22
computers 12, 18, 19, 20, 23, 28, 30, 32, 33
Copperhead 30, 31
crew 21

detector 15, 19, 30
drone 19, 30

8-inch Howitzer M1/M115 35
18-pounder Gun 34
88mm Anti-Aircraft Guns 35
88mm Anti-tank gun Modele 43 38
elevation 6
engine 6, 7, 9, 12, 21
Exocet 17

5.5-inch Medium Gun 37
40mm Bofors Light Anti-Aircraft Gun 35
FH-70 7, 16
FH-77 155mm Howitzer 21
FROG-7 Battlefield Tactical Rocket 43
fuel 6
fuel tanks 6

G5 155mm 21
GCT Howitzer 155 20
gas 6, 24
general support artillery 7, 19
Gepard 29
guidance 6, 8, 9, 10, 11, 12, 13, 14
gunners 7, 23
gunpowder 25
guns 7, 16, 17, 19, 21
gyroscopes 11

HEAT (High Explosive, Anti-Tank) 24, 25
helicopter 26, 27, 29
homing systems 11, 14, 17, 29, 31
HOT Anti-tank Missile 44
howitzers 7, 16, 17, 19, 26, 27

inertial guidance 11, 13
infrared 11, 14, 19, 29

jetevator 9

Lance 6
lasers 11, 18, 30
Light Gun 26, 27

M-47 Dragon 14
M56 26, 27
M102 26, 27
machine guns 18
Maneuverable Independently-Targeted Re-Entry Vehicle (MIRV) 13
Milan Anti-tank Missile 15, 43
Missile System BGM-71A (TOW) 44
Missile System FIM-92A (Stinger) 18, 44
Missile System MGM-5A (Corporal) 42
Missile System MGM-52A (Lance) 44
Missile System MIM-14A (Nike Hercules) 43
Multiple Launch Rocket System (MLRS) 30
muzzle brake 7

105mm Howitzer M1/M101 36
105mm Howitzer M102 27, 40
105mm Light Field Howitzer Model 18 35
105mm Light Field Howitzer Model 43 38
105mm Light Gun L118A1 40
122mm Field Gun D-74 38
122mm Howitzer D-30 39
122mm Howitzer M1938 37
130mm Field Gun M46 39
150mm heavy Field Howitzer Model 18 37
152mm Gun-Howitzer M37 37
155mm Bofors Howitzer FH-77 39
155mm FH-70 Howitzer 7, 41
155mm Gun GPF Mle 34
155mm Gun M1/M59 36
155mm Gun Modele TR 41
155mm Howitzer G5 40
155mm Howitzer M1/M114 36
155mm Howitzer M198 40
155mm Self-propelled Gun GCT 41
155mm Self-propelled Howitzer M109 40
175mm Self-propelled Gun M107 41
OTO-Melara 105mm Model 56 Pack Howitzer 39

pack gun 26
parachute 26, 30
Pershing 8, 12

radar 11, 12, 18, 19, 24, 28, 29, 30, 31
radio 11, 19, 20, 23, 29, 30
Rapier Air Defense Missile 29, 42
RDX 24
recoil system 7, 34
Redeye 14, 15
Re-Entry Vehicle 13
rifles 18
rockets 8, 9, 12, 15, 19, 30
Roland Air Defense Missile 44

75mm Anti-tank gun Model 40 37
75mm Gun Modele 34
75mm Pack Howitzer M8/M116 34
76mm Divisional Gun M1942 38
SA-2 "Guideline" Air Defense Missile 42

SA-4 Gavel 29
SA-8 "Gecko" Air Defense Missile 44
Scud 16
Self-propelled (SP) gun 20
Sergeant York 28, 29
Sexton Self-propelled 25-powder Gun 35
silos 12
smoke shell 24, 25
Space warfare 32
Stinger see Missile System F M-92A
strategic missiles 12, 13
submarines 12
sub-munition shell 24
sustainer 12
Swingfire 8, 9
Swingfire Anti-tank Missile 43

3.7-inch Anti-Aircraft Gun 36
12-inch Howitzer 34
25-pounder Field Gun 36
210mm Railway Gun Model 12 38
tactical guided missile 6, 19
Thrust Vector Control 8, 9
TNT 24
Tomahawk 8
TOW 14
turbofan engine 8
TV cameras 10, 11, 19

V-1 Missile (FZG-76) 33, 42
V-2 33

warhead 6, 12, 13, 15, 30, 31
Wasserfall Air Defense Missile 42
weather 23
wire guidance 11, 14

PRINTED IN BELGIUM BY
**proost**
INTERNATIONAL BOOK PRODUCTION